THE EARTH IS FLAT?!

AND OTHER THINGS MY MOTHER TAUGHT ME

SUSAN HUCKLE

CONTENTS

This book is dedicated to my parents,
John and Dawn Huckle,
who always encouraged me to write.

Whoops.

PROLOGUE

"YOU CAN FOOL all the people some of the time and some of the people all the time, but you cannot fool all the people all the time."

-Abraham Lincoln

(supposedly)

~33~

"I mean, how can people be so stupid?" a balding blonde actor in a blue suit says, throwing up his hands, his face full of scorn.

Ouch.

"What a bunch of idiots!" says a short, spectacled hipster in a raspy voice.

That one always hurts, too.

Talk of conspiracy theories at the other end of the table pricks my ears, stirring a vortex of thrill and dread at my friend Annie's birthday party. It's a typical L.A. gathering of extroverted actors and self-loathing comedians at a loud, all-wood, barrel-shaped bar in the valley.

I used to be a Bible trivia buff. Now my parents have turned me into an expert in global machinations, which makes me entertaining on the outside and a complete wreck on the inside.

Seated across the table from me, Annie's eyes flash with excitement from behind her long brown bangs while her friends mock the online crazies.

"Susan's mom is a flat earther," she says, pointing to me, with an eager grin.

Record scratch.

I down the rest of my Jameson.

Expressions switch to shock, delight, or hesitation. I look normal enough with my nice girl face, long blonde hair, and petite frame, wearing an all Target ensemble of jeans, purple sweater, and boots, but with a flat-earther for a mother, how crazy am I?

"You're joking," the actor says, eyeing me cautiously.

"Get outta here!" the hipster says nasally, his eyes wide.

"No! Not really, though, right?" says a doe-eyed brunette who's been quiet until now.

"Yup, she wholeheartedly believes it," I say with a sigh. "She believes a lot of conspiracy theories, so this fits right into her worldview that there's a global agenda to hide the truth." I try to present the facts as impartially as possible, just like my lawyer father would.

How did he, a usually intelligent, educated, and reasonable man, get suckered into this one?

Life's always been on the fringe with the Huckles: seeking healers, preparing for the End Times, speaking in tongues, but we've been on the outermost edge since about 2014, when the YouTube rabbit hole of rabbit holes sucked my mom in. It's one thing when we clash over my parents' old-fashioned views from the 1950s. It's another when the view is from the 0050s.

"But why are they hiding this?" says the brunette, her brow furrowed.

"And who? And how can she ignore all the proof that it's not flat?" says the hipster, crinkling his nose to adjust his glasses.

Ah, the typical questions. I've fielded them countless times from inquisitive acquaintances, and they were mine, too.

To be heard over the other 30-somethings at the bar bemoaning how their parents ruined their lives, I increase my volume, roll up my sleeves, and explain to my rapt audience:

"She would say NASA is a cover-up for running drugs for top government officials, always Democrats, of course, but it's the Jesuits who really run the world. She would say there's proof of a flat earth in books she's read, but she would mostly point to some Bible verses, like this one about the four corners of the Earth. She believes the Bible is the literal Word of God after all. She would also say that the flight patterns of planes support a flat earth model, so 'the pilots are all in on it.'" I indicate her words with air quotes.

Everyone stares at me, dumbfounded.

Hey, at least your parents have given you some killer party material, Susan.

My friends are dying to meet the conspiracy theorists, either for a laugh or to debate them, but I'm too protective of my parents and fearful of conflict to bring anyone around.

All at once, everyone in earshot at the bar shouts scientific facts about the globe at me as if I don't already know them or haven't mentioned them to my mom already. They have the same self-assured conviction my mom has.

"Yeah, I know, but she just doesn't buy it," I say with a shrug.

"What other conspiracy theories does she believe? 9/11? The moon landing?" says the actor, rolling his eyes.

"She's probably into aliens and lizard people, too, right?" the hipster says, excitedly.

"Yes, and yes," I say, pointing to the actor. "No, and no," I say, pointing to the hipster. "If it's not in the Bible, like aliens or lizard people, it's out."

Time for my new finale.

"Remember the solar eclipse last year? I casually told her

how that phenomenon fits with the sphere model and asked if there was a flat earth explanation. She said-"

I prep my fingers for air quotes again.

"'They're working on it.'"

Now the brunette is agape, and the men are laughing uproariously. It's only a matter of time before each of them will message me the "If the Earth were flat, cats would have pushed everything off of it by now" meme depicting a cartoon cat batting a bottle over the edge of a flat earth in space. If I had a nickel.

I wish I could spend five amusing minutes of my life on this, then go my merry way.

Instead, my disbelief is challenged every time I do my monthly day trip to visit my parents in Santa Barbara, although Mom has uncharacteristically canceled on me the last few months.

"So, how much are you auditioning these days, Evan? My agent sucks," the actor says to the hipster, and the tired conversation about stalled acting careers and "what's your brand?" absorbs the group's attention.

Meanwhile, I'm stuck in the dark abyss of unresolved feelings that I try to drown out by staying busy with acting jobs and outdoor adventures. The thoughts that go unspoken to my mother scream like headlines, center stage of my brain:

Mom, you are out of your damn mind! How can you be so easily taken in? Don't you see how this insane belief lumps you in with the world's worst idiots? I don't want to see you that way! I want to understand where you're coming from, even if I disagree, but this is too much! I'm terrified that I was raised by people who are Christians just because of their extreme gullibility! I trusted you over my own instincts for so long, but my whole life has been one long, slow burn realization that everything you taught me is bananas. Now I don't know what or who to believe!

At the end of the night, I hug the birthday girl goodbye, and just when I start toward the exit, the doe-eyed brunette in an elegant white jumpsuit stops me.

"Thanks for sharing all that about your mom. Wow, that's got to be so hard," she says, and I appreciate the empathy I see in her eyes.

"Yeah, but people certainly deal with worse," I deflect, checking my privilege. At some point, everyone realizes their parents are only human.

At least they love me. Or, rather, they love the lie I present to them.

I know I'm to blame for shattering the tight-knit family unit we used to be. My persona is Little Miss Independent, Miss Never Wants to Get Married and Have Kids, so why am I fundamentally undone by our disconnection over religion, politics, and the fucking shape of the Earth?

"What I'm curious about is why she believes it at all," the brunette says. Godlessness is the L.A. default, so anything else makes Angelinos quizzical. Her eyes search my face for answers while most of the party trickles out into the L.A. evening chill.

Ah, the million-dollar question: why do any of us believe what we do?

"How much time do you have?" I joke.

She laughs, and we get our phones out and exchange contact info in hopes of defying the Hollywood tradition of saying, "Let's get together sometime!" and then not.

That's when I see an email from Mom canceling my next visit.

ACT 1

The "Other Things My Mother Taught Me" Part

CHAPTER 1
THE PATH TO
THE FLAT EARTH

"BUT OF THAT day and hour, no one knows…Therefore you also be ready, for the Son of Man is coming at an hour you do not expect."

-Matthew 24:36-44

~9~

I'm giggling alone in the grocery store, a nine-year-old with a rainbow lollipop and a plan.

It cracks Mom up when I imitate how cheap Grandma is by looking at a price tag, then, no matter what it says, dramatically saying, "39 cents? Too much!" and stomping away. My other big hit is walking with one stiff leg and shouting, "I got jet leg! I got jet leg!" I know it's jet lag, but I'll do anything to hear her big, loud laugh.

Wearing my favorite outfit, a faded red shirt with a white whale on it and denim culottes, while my strawberry blonde ponytail bounces with anticipation, I hold the lollipop up high for my joke and look around for Mom, but she's nowhere in sight.

Uh, oh. Where is she?

I go to the end of the aisle and look right, then left. I know to never ever ever make a scene, so I try to hide my fear and calmly but thoroughly search the store. I know instantly, though, the most likely explanation: she has been raptured.

The Rapture, when all the Christians instantly disappear from Earth and go to heaven, is all we talk about at church and at home, because it could be any day now (like right...NOW!). Mom, Dad, and I are good fundamentalist Pentecostal Christians, so we believe the Book of Revelation in the Bible is about the End Times: the Rapture, the Tribulation (when the bad people are punished), and Jesus's 1,000-year reign on Earth. It's obvious the End Times are near because of how bad and crazy everyone is now in the 1990s, even in our boring town in California. People aren't dressing and acting the way they're supposed to, and women want to kill their babies.

I guess I wasn't a good enough Christian to be raptured?

Tears well up in my eyes. The guilt is too much.

When was the last time I prayed? Maybe yesterday? If only I had been a better Christian! I would be with my parents now in heaven!

I picture them backlit by the sun, glowing in white robes, step touching in a huge choir, even though Dad doesn't sing.

God, if by some miracle, you haven't done the Rapture yet, I promise I will be good! I will never ever ever give you a reason to not rapture me!

Then a wave of panic makes my heart beat faster.

How am I going to survive THE TRIBULATION?! The drawings in our End Times books of lakes of fire, plagues, and flying men on horses are terrifying!

Whenever I have a test coming up or a shot at the doctor's, I make Mom laugh by looking up at the sky and joking, "Rapture me, Lord!" But it's not a joke now as I start a sweaty second lap around the grocery store.

I believe in Jesus with my whole heart, but sometimes I drop my Flintstones vitamins into the plant near my chair at the kitchen table because they're yucky.

Is that why I wasn't raptured?

"Cashier to register four," a bored employee says over the loudspeaker while I stumble through the produce maze.

How did I miss the warning signs, though?

My parents aren't sure yet if Bill Clinton is the Antichrist or if the Mark of the Beast has started, which Revelation says will doom someone to Hell if they accept it. The Mark of the Beast sounds like a scratch you get from a scary bear, but my parents say it could be a tattoo, anything "implanted under the skin," or credit cards.

Then it hits me. I almost drop the lollipop.

Wouldn't everyone notice if all the Christians just disappeared? Wouldn't cars be running into each other, and people be screaming for their friends who were just there a minute ago?

I excitedly walk back down the aisles looking for piles of clothes that should be on the ground where a Christian was raptured. That was in a movie we watched at church.

Everyone looks calm in the store, and I don't see any piles of clothes!

Maybe the Rapture hasn't happened yet!

I squint at the checkout lanes, and at the farthest one, there she is. I practically fall to the ground with relief.

Thank you, God, thank you, thank you!

She's smiling and writing a check, her fluffy, blonde hair stiff with hairspray, while four paper bags sit in her shopping cart. Her colorful satin dress with shoulder pads up to her ears hugs her big butt and should have made her easier to find.

She's dressed up because tonight she's going to give her testimony, the story of how she became a Christian, at church. I'm not allowed to go because something in her testimony is "not appropriate" for me to hear, so of course I want to hear it!

I walk to her while I pray.

Dear God, thank you so much for not doing the Rapture yet. I will be a better Christian from now on. I love you so much. Amen.

When I pray, I picture a peaceful old man in a long white

robe with long white hair and a long white beard. Light shines from behind him, and I feel warm and safe.

"Find anything you want?" she asks me cheerfully as I take my place by her side.

I look down at the lollipop still in my tight fist, but I'm in no mood to do my joke. I set it down with the candy bars at the checkout lane and shake my head to say "no," hoping I look normal and not like I was about to cry.

I will never lose her again.

———

After we get home and put the groceries away, I walk through our small, dark wood-paneled den, which is exploding with Bibles and books about the Bible. I tiptoe around the piles of Sandi Patty and Crystal Gayle tapes to get to my room to draw. I won an award in school for my drawing of a baby giraffe standing on its mother's back to eat the leaves on a tall tree.

I freeze when I hear the sound of rattling papers and Mom nervously pacing in the next room.

"My name is Dawn Huckle, and this is my testimony," she says with a shaky voice under her breath.

Oh! Maybe I can catch whatever is "not appropriate" for me to hear in her testimony while she practices it!

I hold my breath so I can hear better and stay frozen so she can't tell I'm in earshot.

"I was living in Santa Barbara in the '70s when I was handed a tract of the Gospel of John on the street," she whispers slowly. "At the time, I was in my 30s, single, had just lost my father to cancer, and was working at the welfare department."

I hear her pencil nervously scribble something out, then she continues.

"The Truth in that tract hit me like a bolt of lightning, and I immediately joined the church and started studying the Bible. I excitedly shared the Good News with my roommates and co-workers, but they didn't want to hear it. I ended up losing all of my friends." She sighs. She always looks sad when she talks about her old Santa Barbara friends.

"I know now that I had been looking for God my whole life, but in all the wrong places. At one point, I was part of a Satanic cult…"

My eyes bug, and my heart stops.

A Satanic CULT?

I picture Mom as she looks in old photos: thin with long, shiny blonde '70s hair, but dressed in black and part of a circle of other women in black dresses in the woods at night.

Witches!

Something is in the middle of the circle.

A steaming cauldron? A bloody animal? Some other sacrifice to Satan?

The scene is scary but kind of exciting, too.

Mom always says, "Daddy was the sweet sinner, and I was the bad sinner," meaning he didn't do anything too bad before he became a Christian, but she did.

This must be what she's talking about!

"At a certain point, you come to the end of yourself, and that's where I was when He found me…" she continues, but her words fade into the background while cult images parade through my brain.

I stare at the den's wall-length bookcase that has an eye-level shelf devoted to End Times prophecy books like *The Late Great Planet Earth* and dramatic Tribulation fiction like the *Left Behind* series with all their fiery, apocalyptic images.

Thank goodness Mom's not part of a cult anymore!

CHAPTER 2
THE DEVIL'S LOOSE ON THE FLAT EARTH

"BE ALERT...YOUR enemy the Devil prowls around like a roaring lion looking for someone to devour."
   -1 Peter 5:8

~10~

With my ear pressed to my parents' white closed door and my Malt-O-Meal breakfast digesting in my stomach, I listen for Mom to start her shower. When I hear her open the bathroom door, I feel giddy and tingly with anticipation.

Almost time…

I hear the shriek of the knob twisting, then water running.

…now!

Time to do my one bad thing.

I race across the thick, tan carpet to the den, our recently converted library-turned-homeschooling spot.

My 4th grade teacher last year at my Christian elementary school, Mrs. Dowling, a.k.a. "Scowlin' Dowlin'," who looked like a linebacker in Easter dresses, made fun of my cursive in front of the whole class. As soon as I told Mom about it, she unenrolled me, bought the Christian curriculum the school uses, and we started homeschooling. School's always been easy for me, so she soon realized she could simply tear out each subject's daily assignment and leave me to it by myself.

With a sly grin, my heart pounding, and one ear listening for her shower to stop, I go to the cubby under the brown desk where all the teacher's manuals are. They're out in the open, in my defense.

I grab the heavy, green spiral-bound science one, my least favorite subject, and find the answer key to today's assignment. Standing over the desk, I quickly but carefully fill in the answers on my sheet.

First question: "Who created the Earth?"

Answer key: "God. Other acceptable answers: Jesus, Jesus Christ, the Holy Spirit."

C'mon, so easy. Only an idiot doesn't know that.

Second question: "How long did it take to create the Earth?"

Answer key: "Six days."

That one's tricky, but I remember God rested on the seventh day.

Third question: "How old is the Earth?"

Answer key: "About 6,000 years."

Essay question: "Science relies on evidence. Using complete sentences, please give 2-3 examples of evidence for the Earth's age."

The answer key lists many options, so I choose three and put them into my own words to throw Mom off the scent. I write: "The Bible covers about 6,000 years. There was only a little dust when we landed on the moon, so it can't be very old. Carbon dating shows rocks aren't very old either."

I put that teacher's manual away in the cubby and fish out the thick, orange spiral bound history one, my second least favorite subject. While my lower back teeth ache from the bands I wear at night on my braces to fix my overbite, I realize the shower water isn't running anymore.

Oh, no! How long has it been off? Is she about to walk in?

I listen for footsteps. I was only spanked a few times for

pulling the cat's tail when I was little, but whatever the punishment would be for cheating, nothing would hurt as much as her disappointment.

"Susan!" Mom calls from her room. "What do you want to do for lunch today?"

I hear her sit down at her squeaky vanity table. My heartbeat slows. It'll take her a while to put on her 'war paint,' as Grandma Spencer, my mom's mom, calls makeup.

"Let's do Taco Bell!" I squeak through my metal mouth.

It's our favorite. Last week, we died laughing when she opened a packet of their mild sauce, and it squirted across the table and all over my lavender sweater.

I continue copying the answers to my history assignment while I fantasize about all the fun things I can do as soon as my school work is done. I can look for frogs and lizards in the backyard, play the piano, swim at the YMCA, or d) all of the above! I'm not cheating because I don't know the answers, but to get this child's play over with and get to the fun!

In the middle of an essay about how the Spanish missions in California helped the Indians become Christians, I hear the creak of her vanity table.

Time's up, Susan! Hurry!

I carefully but quickly put the history teacher's manual away exactly how it was before, then plop on the carpet with my legs splayed wide around our squishy mustard ottoman and continue writing my essay on top of it: "The Spanish taught the Indians about Jesus at the missions. Many Indians were saved and grateful..."

"I got this for your sleepover next week," Mom sings, walking into the den carrying a fuzzy, pink sleeping bag with lambs on it. She's gone from housewife to plus-size model in her red turtleneck, black stretchy jeans, and chunky shoes.

"Oh, thanks, Mom," I say, keeping my head down. My parents are on a "you need to make friends!" kick, but as an only child used to being around adults, I can't stand being around children.

She sits in the mustard recliner in front of me, clasps her hands together, and purses her lips.

"Now, Susan, listen to me. This is very important."

The seriousness of her tone activates my nervous system, which often happens between dramatic prophecies in church and Biblical revelations at home on the daily. I put my pencil down and give her my full attention.

"If anyone ever pulls out a Ouija board at a sleepover, you call me immediately. Get out of that house RIGHT AWAY. Those are very dangerous. You have no idea what sorts of demonic spirits you could summon."

Yikes. Sounds like she had a bad experience.

"Okay, Mom," I say, then she leaves the room. I look back down at my assignment, but I can't concentrate. The chances of me actually encountering a Ouija board seem slim to none since the only kids I know are through church. I've never seen a Ouija board, but I picture a board game like our favorites, Monopoly or Sorry, but with ghosts floating out of it.

Or do you just talk to the ghosts?

Why would anyone want to do that?

———

The next day, my parents invite Tessa from church over to play after our soccer games. We're often confused for sisters with our matching blonde hair and big smiles, but she's two years younger than me and is such a child. I have to do all the heavy lifting when we play.

With aching calves, heads covered in dried sweat, and still in our jerseys, we hit my happy place: my big backyard that has a magnolia tree in the center with a swing, an apricot tree that you can't eat the fruit from for some reason, and a playhouse.

"Now let's ride and explore!" I have my Barbie say to Tessa's

Barbie. Then I bend her legs to sit on this iridescent horse I love, gearing up for a lap around the backyard.

"But I don't have a horse," Tessa has her Barbie say to mine, looking at me with helpless green eyes.

Ugh, do I have to do everything?

I'm about to begrudgingly suggest her Barbie join mine on *my* horse when Mom starts scream-praying in the living room.

"JESUS, help us! JESUS, save him! JESUS, have mercy on him! JESUS, be with me! Jesus! Jesus! JESUS!"

Tessa looks at me wide-eyed.

Man, Mom can be embarrassing.

I look through the screen door and see her pacing back and forth, waving her arms wildly, and shaking her head as she cries out.

"Oh, she's always like that," I say with an eye roll. She flies off the handle all the time and blames it on menopause. We're always stopping at Jack in the Box so she can get an extra-large iced tea for her hot flashes. She had me at 42 and hates when people think I'm her granddaughter.

"Okay, you can ride with me this time, but you should really get your own horse," I have my Barbie say to Tessa's Barbie. Then Mom tears open the screen door.

"Tessa, your mom is coming to pick you up. Get your stuff together," she says gruffly, then she looks at me. "Something's happened to Daddy."

My stomach drops. She slams the screen door and goes back to scream-praying.

"JESUS, be with us! JESUS, we believe in you! JESUS…"

Tessa looks at me with a don't-you-feel-badly-about-that-eye-roll-now look, then I walk to the side of the backyard and peer into Dad's room through the bay window. My heart pounds loudly in my ears as my eyes adjust from the brightness outside to the dim of his room.

I see his body lying on the ground at the foot of his bed on one side, his face turned toward the bed's white comforter, so I can't see it.

"Dad, are you ok?" I ask timidly through the window.

"I'm fine, Susan. Everything's fine," he says from the floor, calm as can be.

But it doesn't look like he can move.

I have no idea what to do!

Tessa's mom picks her up, and I go to my room to hide from whatever is happening. Meanwhile, Mom's voice grows hoarse from praying in tongues in the living room.

"Oh, shadadadabadada, shadadadabada! Oooooh, shadadadabada…"

This is serious.

Sitting on my bed, with my door ajar, I see paramedics walk by, and minutes later, they pass again with Dad on a stretcher, his blank face drooping to one side.

I know I should pray or help or cry, but I just sit there like a pillar of salt.

CHAPTER 3
REVELATIONS ON THE FLAT EARTH

"YOU RESTORED me to health and let me live. Surely it was for my benefit that I suffered such anguish."
-Isaiah 38:16

~10~

I feel like I'm waking up from a deep, no-dreams sleep.

How long have I been out?

Mom's driving us to the hospital, and it's the first time I'm seeing Dad since he was removed on that stretcher a month ago. I can't remember anything since then. I look out the window at the super sunny day, suburban homes, and shopping centers we pass, and squint.

Has the world always been this bright?

"Daddy's excited to see you," Mom says to me with a big smile in the rear-view mirror.

I don't believe her. He's quiet and serious like his parents, Grandma and Grandpa Huckle. I know I should have missed him and be looking forward to this, but I'm not.

In the backseat, in my white dress with blue roses on it and a big white bow in my hair, I sit still and try to piece together the words whispered outside my bedroom door and on the phone over the last month: "left-side paralysis," "hereditary high blood pressure," "blood vessel burst," "stroke."

Did he have a stroke because the soccer games that morning, mine and Tessa's, were too much for his blood pressure? Is this my fault?

"Daddy almost died that first night in the hospital," Mom says while we sit at a stoplight.

I think she's trying to explain why I should be happy instead of scared.

"But so many people from church came. We prayed all night for God to intercede and save his life, and He did!"

Where was I? I can't remember.

I picture people from our church in a circle in a waiting room scream-praying, just like they do at prayer meetings, with sweaty faces and strained voices: "We bring John before you, Father God! He loves you, Father God! Please, show your mercy and save him! His work is not done on this earth! He is your vessel, Lord God!"

"He should be stable enough to start physical therapy soon so he can walk again," Mom adds hopefully. I nod but keep looking at the sky through the window and start to pray with my eyes open.

Dear God, I don't understand. Why did this happen to my dad? He's a perfect Christian. He goes to church every Sunday. He prays every day, and he reads his Bible all the time. He never gets mad or uses bad words. He doesn't do any bad things for his body, like smoke or drink. He doesn't eat red meat and never has dessert, unlike Mom and me. And he jogs almost every day!

Sometimes I jog with him to the strawberry fields on the outskirts of town, and when I get tired, we just walk, smelling the eucalyptus trees that line the fields and crunching their seed caps under our feet.

As we near the hospital, we pass the unusual white and teal Victorian cottage that has a pink neon sign in the window that says "Psychic readings."

Oh, boy, here we go.

It catches Mom's eye as it always does, and she shakes her head and yells like clockwork, "We rebuke you in Jesus' name! Get out of Santa Maria! You have no stronghold here!"

It's scary when she yells like that, and I don't understand how she can be so mad at someone we don't know.

We park and take the elevator. Everyone seems stressed in this unfamiliar, cold place. Mom holds my hand tightly and drags me to his room.

"Look who's here!" she says as we walk through the door.

"Hi, Susan," Dad says.

He looks tired. He sits in the bed with his faded hospital gown twisted and normally military-short dark hair longer than usual. He doesn't move his body at all.

This is not how he's supposed to look. Everything is not how it's supposed to be.

The fluorescent lighting is dim, and the tall machines around him look like gray ghosts.

Are there demons in here?

We talk about spiritual warfare, demonic spirits, and Satan being "up to no good" so much so that I always wonder what's around me in the spirit world that I can't see.

Remember, Susan, God is in control. He'll fix this in no time.

"He missed you," Mom says, filling the silence.

She always knows what to say, but Dad and I have to think first. She nudges me to say something or move closer, but I stay quiet at the foot of his bed. All I can think about are the things he can't do anymore, like play tennis, his favorite, or save me from mean dogs like the one that chased me when I was five and put its jaw around my neck.

I think our jogs in the strawberry fields are over.

———

The next morning, Mom looks as white as her robe as we eat breakfast at our small kitchen table surrounded by yellow wallpaper with red chickens. She hasn't straightened her hair yet, so it's a rare sighting of her short natural tight curls, which I think are so pretty, but she hates. Her gray-blue eyes have a faraway look in them.

"God spoke to me in a dream last night," she says.

I nearly drop my English muffin.

Stop the presses! This is BIBLICAL!

"God said these words to me, clear as a bell: 'I will raise him up on the third day.'"

Third day. I get it. Like Jesus.

In my Lion King sleep shirt, I feel our usually skittish gray cat Snickle rub on my leg and purr.

"Daddy is going to walk again," she explains.

Right, cause yesterday the doctor said Dad will learn to walk with a cane through physical therapy.

"God is going to heal him," she says, now with determination in her eyes.

The red chickens on the wall do a double-take.

"Oh," I say, raising my eyebrows.

We don't know anybody who's been healed, but I know it happened in the Bible. I want to ask how she can be sure she heard from God, but I don't want to make her mad.

How do you know the difference between God and your own thoughts?

I remember when I was five and thought there was barely any milk left in the jug to pour over my cereal. But then milk kept pouring out, more than enough for my bowl of cereal, and I thought, "It's a miracle!" I've wondered since, though, if I just didn't eyeball correctly how much was left.

"Remember that time I felt an angel take the wheel and save us from getting into an accident? I felt the same way last night," she says, recalling an incident I was too young to remember but know because she references it a lot.

"We are going to hold onto this promise from God, okay?" she says, taking my hand.

My parents know everything about God and the Bible, so I take their word for it.

"Okay," I say, through a mouthful of buttery, sugary, cinnamon-y English muffin.

I start to fantasize about God healing Dad: him walking again, my family telling everyone at church, people believing in Jesus because of it, and us jogging in the strawberry fields!

But what if it doesn't happen?

Then I panic, wondering if God's hurt when I doubt Him.

I'm so sorry, God! Of course, I trust in You!

Snickle jumps onto my lap, and her purrs vibrate my thighs while her fur tickles my skin. I hug her tightly while Mom clears the table.

Dear God, thank you so much for raising my dad up on the third day. That will be so amazing. I will pray as much as I can to make this happen. Amen.

CHAPTER 4
FLAT EARTH TO SUSAN

"WOULD you be free from the burden of sin?
   There's pow'r in the blood, pow'r in the blood;
   Would you o'er evil a victory win?
   There's wonderful pow'r in the blood."
-Hymn by John. E Lewis

~11~

The morning sun illuminates every corner of my purple-everywhere room when I pull my Animaniacs panties down and see a tablespoon of blood in the center.

Uh, oh, am I dying?

I have a great trick for scary moments like these: just forget it happened!

I bury the telling underwear deep in my white wicker hamper, so Mom won't be alarmed when she does laundry, and hope for the best.

Maybe it'll just go away.

I put on clean underwear, black leggings, and a tan T-shirt from Vacation Bible School (a week-long summer Bible party at church for kids) and head to the living room for my first day of sixth grade.

Mom, in a floral top and white jeans, is fiddling with the TV.

"This year, Susan, we're going to try video schooling!" she chirps, her eyes beaming through her big, clear glasses.

Huh?

"Each videotape is about half a school day, so I've put the first one in. You just have to hit 'Play.' The rest are here, and they're in order and labeled," she says, pointing to the box of VHS tapes next to our TV. "This Christian school in Pensacola filmed a full year of lessons in their classroom! Isn't that neat?"

Is she onto the fact that I've been cheating? I don't see the teacher's manuals anywhere.

"Okay, I have a full day, so I'll leave you to it." She spends two days a week visiting Dad at rehab, an hour away, where he has full-time physical therapy to learn how to walk again (no healing yet). The facility is called Solutions, but we laugh at Grandma Spencer for always calling it 'Solitudes.'

At least his roommate there, a 20-year-old who was badly injured when he drunkenly crashed his car, is quieter than his roommate in the hospital, a white-haired old man who constantly, weakly shouted, "Help! Gimme help!" At home, Mom and I jokingly imitate him, but I actually find him really sad.

I warily hit 'Play' on the VCR and sit cross-legged on the carpet.

"Hi, there! Welcome to 6th grade. I'm Miss Collins, and I'm going to be your teacher for the year," a tan, perky woman with long, curly blonde hair says in between giggles in front of a green chalkboard. The students, my fellow 6th graders, I guess, are just out of frame and seem to be snickering, too.

Why are they laughing? What did I miss?

"Let's start class like we do every day: with prayer. Everyone, bow your heads and close your eyes. Father God, we thank you for this day together. Help us to be good students…"

Watching this VIDEO is going to waste so much time! I have movie star biographies from the library to read and show tunes to play on the piano!

Then Mom marches into the room holding my bloody underwear with one hand and a plastic package in the other. Her mood has completely changed, but I can't put my finger on what it is.

Am I dying?

Am I in trouble?

Just tell me!

"I found these when I started doing laundry just now," she says sternly, holding up the underwear. "This is a period, Susan. It'll happen every month for a week, and when it does, you put these pads in your underwear." She holds up the plastic package, explains how they work, and sends me to the bathroom to put one on.

She seems upset, almost as mad as that one time I thought it would be fun to ride down the stairs in the laundry basket and tumbled down instead. Have I done something wrong?

In the bathroom, I fumble with sticking the wings of the pad around my–

Wait.

My body does WHAT?

How have I never heard of this before? God, can you heal periods, too?

I waddle back to the living room with what feels like a pillow between my legs and resume video schooling until Mom leaves to visit Dad.

The second she's gone, a burst of energy hits me.

I race to my closet and change into my favorite dress: an old-fashioned, white, lacy number that I love twirling in because the long skirt comes up so high. It makes me feel like the lead of one of my favorite movie musicals we rent from the library: *Follow the Fleet, Babes in Arms,* or *On the Town.* In those movies, everyone is beautiful, funny, and blissfully unaware of the End Times.

Like a dancer making her entrance, I return to the living room, push the coffee table to the side, and replace Miss Collins with *Top Hat* in the VCR. I fast forward to my favorite number and sing and dance along, my favorite thing to do when I have the house to myself.

My imagination turns the flowery pastel sofa, tan carpet, and dark wood walls that I'm dancing in front of into a huge theatre with blinding stage lights and a full audience in the dark. This is when I feel most alive. I don't even feel the pillow between my legs anymore.

Then I freeze mid-spin when a horrible thought smacks me back to being an 11-year-old in an old-timey dress dancing for no one in an ordinary living room.

What if right now I just dropped to the ground, paralyzed? My dreams of actually singing and dancing on a stage would be over.

I know now that everything can change in a moment.

God, you wouldn't let that happen to me, right? I know you created me and love me so much that you sent your only Son to die for my sins. John 3:16!

An uncomfortable reality gnaws at me, though.

But...you did let it happen to my dad...

From the TV, Fred Astaire's soft voice pulls me back into my fantasy.

I close my eyes and pretend that he and I are dancing in front of an adoring crowd. He loves me, we magically know the steps, and I feel better.

It's not till later, when I hear Mom pull into the driveway and race to my room to change, that I notice the blood stains on the inner lining of my white dress.

CHAPTER 5
CRACKS IN THE FLAT EARTH

"PRAISE THE LORD, my soul, and forget not all his benefits: who forgives all your sins, and heals all your diseases…"
-Psalms 103:2-3

~12~

In a stretchy black and white dress, white stockings, and blue glasses, my lumpy 12-year-old body slumps into the couch while Dad and I wait for Mom to get ready for church. We're seeing our umpteenth traveling faith healer and hoping today's the day God makes good on his promise to heal Dad of his left side paralysis.

On the TV, Benny Hinn, the televangelist, races down the line of people at his altar shouting, "Jesus! Jesus! Jesus!" and tapping a different person's forehead on every "Jesus," making them fall backwards. His staff of tall, strong men in black suits can barely keep up with catching each person and laying them down as Benny knocks them over with the Holy Ghost.

How do we know these people are actually getting healed? What if they were faking being sick?

"I am healed in Jesus' name…in Jesus' name…in Jesus' name.

Isaiah 53:5: 'By his stripes, we are healed,'" Dad, in puffy black slacks and a navy jacket, meditates under his breath with a strained face as he slowly walks laps with his cane through the living room and the den.

Our bookcase is overflowing now with biographies about famous healers like Kathryn Kuhlman and John G. Lake, binders of printed-out healing-related Bible verses, and anointed oil from Israel that you make into a cross on the forehead of the person being prayed over. The house smells like pee because sometimes Dad doesn't make it to the bathroom, slowed down in his wheelchair by our thick carpet or by his shaky cane walking. At least the air force base said he can come back to his job as a contract lawyer whenever he's ready.

What if my simmering doubts are keeping God from healing him?

I can't bear being responsible for Dad staying handicapped, so I push my questions aside. My parents drove hours and hours recently to see Benny Hinn at a huge convention center, but there were too many people ahead of them at the altar. The service ended before Benny could pray for him.

Yesterday, I was washing the dishes when I overheard Mom cry to Dad in their room, "I can't do this anymore! I can't handle it! This is TOO MUCH!"

My heart started pounding.

Dear God, please help my parents get through this. Please don't let them get divorced.

I try to help by never bothering them with anything.

"Okay, let's get going," Mom barks, rushing into the living room.

In a long, light blue dress, she grabs her huge purse, and we all head to the garage to get in the car. She shoves a few chocolate pinwheels into her mouth from a box on the kitchen counter on the way. Then she firmly holds Dad's limp left arm to steady him as he slowly and cautiously swings his stiff left leg down a step to the garage level, shuffles it until he feels secure, plants his cane strategically, then steps down with his right leg. It's another slow, careful process to get him into the passenger's seat. Mom treats Dad like fragile china now, going from zero to heart attack over any false step.

As I get in the backseat, Mom hurls his emergency, heavy, black metal wheelchair into the trunk and screams, "We reject this wheelchair! We reject this paralysis! We reject it in Jesus' name!" She slams the trunk, and off to church we go.

This church meets in an industrial space, so it feels more like a business meeting. In a navy suit, today's faith healer is built like a baseball player and is younger and more soft-spoken than the loud, arrogant healers we watch on my parents' favorite station: TBN, Trinity Broadcasting Network.

Maybe this guy's the real deal?

"Good morning, my brothers and sisters in Christ. It's a great day to be in the house of the Lord," he says warmly.

A few of the 50 or so churchgoers shout, "Amen!"

My parents get out pens to take notes on the service's program while I quietly sneak some Necco Wafers out of Mom's purse to munch on. I'm too hungry to wait for church breakfast, a.k.a. communion, a.k.a. the body and blood of Christ in cracker and grape juice form.

"I'd like to talk about Psalm 103 today, where God is described as the One who 'heals all our diseases.' Notice that beautiful word, my brothers and sisters." He pauses dramatically. "'All.'"

I hear sniffling and look over at Dad, who has tears streaming down his face. I never saw him cry before his stroke, but now he does a lot. The doctor said this is common for stroke patients. Dad balled when he received a handmade Get Well Soon card from my 3rd grade teacher, Mrs. Klein, and her class.

After a sermon full of anecdotes about all the healings he's witnessed comes the moment everyone's been waiting for.

"And now, anyone who would like prayer for healing, please come forward," the faith healer says, and about 20 people start to stand.

Dad slowly plods to the front with his cane and Mom assisting him, and they end up between an older man with a large growth on the side of his face and a middle-aged woman with a scarf covering her bald head. I stay in my seat and finish the Neccos. Something like sad hope fills my heart as I watch them wait patiently together, Mom holding Dad's arm and waist to steady him.

The healer gets to Dad and lays a hand on his shoulder while they talk for a minute, then they all bow their heads while he prays. From my seat, I close my eyes, bow my head, and concentrate on healing.

I believe, God. I promise, I believe you can do this.

I imagine Dad throwing his cane and running back down the aisle toward me with a big smile on his face and both hands in the air, even though no apparent healings happened to the people ahead of him.

It could happen right…NOW!

I open my eyes.

Nothing.

I close them again and concentrate harder.

Ooooooor…now!

The healer starts talking to Mom, and I see her mouth the word 'depression' to him. Something about the way she looks up to him and softly answers his questions makes her seem child-like. He lays one hand on her forehead and raises the other to heaven and prays. After a few minutes, my parents walk back to me the same as they'd left.

Man. And I really believed that time.

"How'd it go?" I ask quietly when they sit down next to me, while the rest of the line gets prayed for.

"He said we can come to the evening service tonight for more intense prayer," Mom says casually.

This is the usual line, and my parents never do.

"There aren't too many people here. Why don't you go forward for your eyes?" she adds.

I've had glasses since I was five and figured this was just my destiny since Mom and Dad wear coke bottle thick glasses, too. Before I can reply, she takes my hand and walks us to the back of the line.

"And what would you like prayer for?" the healer asks when it's my turn.

Um, this whole period thing?

With her hands on my shoulders, Mom says, "Could you pray for her to have perfect eyesight?"

"What's your name?" he says, looking down at me. Up close, he's very tall and sweaty.

"Susan," I say softly.

The healer lays his hands on my head. They are large and very hot.

Cause of the Holy Spirit, or is he nervous?

With my hands at my sides, I grab fistfuls of my dress since *I'm* nervous and close my eyes.

"Dear God," he says, full of passionate conviction, "we believe that you can give Sarah here 20/20 vision. You love her and want her to see clearly, in Jesus' name."

He takes his hands off my head.

"Now take your glasses off," he commands, and I do.

He looks around, finds a black-and-white clock on the dark wood wall, and points.

"Now tell everyone the time on that clock," he says confidently.

I squint as hard as I can at the white blur on the wall, but unfortunately for both of us, I can't make out the time.

Maybe I should guess based on how long the service has probably been going on? Would that make everyone happy?

"I can't really see it very well," I stammer, ashamed to let him and everyone down.

He repeats the invitation to his evening service for more prayer, then Mom silently walks us back to get Dad and leave. There's a post-church lunch rush at Red Lobster to beat after all.

Unspoken disappointment lingers after every unsuccessful healing service. Then hope is renewed when they learn of a new healer coming to town, and the cycle continues.

Father God, please heal my dad at the next healing service. He's so deserving. I'm sure it will all make sense someday, why you're taking so long.

CHAPTER 6
FLAT EARTH THEATRE

"HOW BEAUTIFUL ARE the feet of those who preach the gospel of peace, who bring glad tidings of good things!"
    -Romans 10:15

~13~

"People say this show is starting the next big revival," Mom whispers to me eagerly as we take our seats in the balcony of our church. The modern, octagonal building hums with anticipation as well-dressed old ladies gab in pews while tired parents try to wrangle their kids. My sour, teenage face, plastered in acne-hiding foundation, contrasts with her enthusiasm.

We usually sit on the main floor, but our 500-seat church, a First Assemblies of God denomination, is packed tonight for *Heaven's Gate and Hell's Flames*, a dynamite touring show saving souls across the nation. The congregation was told to invite non-believers, but we don't know any, so it's just Mom and me since Dad isn't interested in frivolities like theatre.

"This must be God's last push to save people before the Rapture," she says, dolled up as usual with teased short blonde hair, blue eye shadow-enhanced eyes, pink lipstick, and a loud dress.

Rapture me now, Lord. Since going back to real school for seventh grade, I've never felt more like an alien.

Our church happened to start a small Christian junior high the year I went into 7th grade, so my parents decided to stop homeschooling me and send me there. I think they feared I'd get weird if I stayed isolated from kids my own age.

Too late.

I don't get my fellow 7th graders' references (Britney Spears? Harry Potter? Backstreet Boys?), and they don't get mine (*The Dick Van Dyke Show*? 1930s screwball comedies? MGM musicals? Anybody?). I've never lived down showing up for the first day of school in a purple wrap skirt Mom sewed me with a T-shirt TUCKED INTO IT. The second I got home, I screamed at Mom, "Everyone wears JEANS! I NEED JEANS!"

At the end of the first week, Amy told me that Kelly said I should have never been born.

Ouch, Amy. Why would you tell me that?

"Do you see anyone from school?" Mom asks cheerily, looking around.

"Yeah, Tiffany, Christy, Kelly, and Amanda are sitting together down there," I say, pointing.

Their bouncy, shiny, curled hair and skinny bodies in tight, cute dresses caught my eye as soon as we walked in. I'm too self-conscious about my ENORMOUS hips and butt (thanks, Mom) to wear anything tight, and I don't want to be like everybody else with curling iron ringlets.

They're probably talking about how much fun they had on the class trip to Six Flags that I wasn't allowed to go on.

Mom's convinced I'll die if I step foot on a roller coaster.

In the interest of looking cool, I'm keeping a lid on how excited I am to see real live actors tonight. Theatre is the only thing I want to do. Actors look like they're having so much fun, and they always know what to say. I'd give anything to be that confident and free. I have to complete a long mental checklist before I speak: Is this Godly? Is this nice? Is this correct? Could someone take this the wrong way? Am I sinning? Could I get in trouble? Will this hurt anybody?

The lights dim, the audience politely applauds, and I lean in.

I'll show my classmates when I'm on stage someday.

When the lights come up on the stage, a man with angel wings is praying on the outside of a door. He takes his angel wings off, then enters a teacher's lounge set and pretends to be a new teacher at the school.

But he's really an angel sent from heaven. I get it.

"You're Miss Williams, right?" he says to another teacher, a pretty young woman. "I've heard about you. God wants me to tell you that He loves you."

She breaks down in tears as the angel, pretending to be a new teacher, walks her through the prayer to accept Jesus into her heart. The audience cheers.

She's about to go back to her classroom when she gasps, holds her chest, then drops to the ground, stone cold dead.

Then the upstage stairs and backdrop curtains light up bright white, and from the top of the stairs, God welcomes her to eternity at heaven's gate.

"Jesus! Jesus! I'm so glad to see you!" she says as she runs up the steps into God's arms after dying of a heart attack. God is a young man wearing a Santa beard and a white robe.

"My beloved child! And just in time! Welcome to Heaven!" he bellows, and the gospel music swells while angels celebrate.

The next scene is of a businessman picking up a hitchhiker, who is the angel in disguise again. The hitchhiker/angel tries to share God's love with him, but he rejects it.

I'd want to play the angel. He's in every scene!

"Thanks, but no thanks, pal. I don't need this 'Jesus.' I'm doing just fine without him," the businessman says as he drops the hitchhiker/angel off.

Sitting in a folding chair, the actor playing the businessman mimes continuing to drive, and then the lights indicate head-lights coming right at him.

"Oh, noooooooo!" he cries out.

Blackout. Car crash sound effect.

The lights come up on the upstage steps and curtains, but now everything is in a pool of red, and the Devil is laughing at the top of the steps. He's a stocky man in a red onesie.

"Ahahahahaha! Because of your pride, you're miiiiiiiine! Welcome to Hell!" His enunciation makes every vowel and consonant explode.

The businessman falls to his knees and breaks down.

"No! Jesus, help me! Is it really too late?" He looks devastated at the thought of eternity in Hell.

His acting is so believable!

Lights up on Hell was initially laughable, but now I'm struck by the agony people experience when they wake up in Hell.

Their wrong choice can never be undone!

"You had your chance! Mwahahahaha!" the Devil snarls.

Last Sunday, our pastor interviewed the actor who plays the Devil and asked him how he copes with playing the epitome of evil.

"It takes a lot out of me," he said with a weary face.

The show's pattern continues, showing people either accepting or rejecting the incognito angel's plea for salvation, then dying unexpectedly and facing the consequences of their decisions: joyful eternity with a loving God or eternal torture and damnation with Satan in Hell.

For the finale, the angel, fully decked out in a white robe, wings, and a halo, walks center stage and breaks the fourth wall.

"Now remember, anyone you meet could really be an angel sent from God," he says solemnly. "Keep your heart right with the Lord because you never know when your time on this Earth-"

He raises his hand slowly.

"-is up."

He snaps. Blackout. Decimation.

Weeping echoes throughout the church as the weight of Hell's tragic, irreversible reality stuns the congregation. Mom is aghast while I fantasize about what it would be like to perform in this tour, night after night, playing these dramatic scenes for a spellbound, emotional crowd.

Our pastor takes the stage in a beige suit and green tie, his gut runneth over. He looks like Don Rickles and talks like Red Skelton.

"Wow, one more hand for the company of *Heaven's Gate and Hell's Flames*! Powerful. So powerful. And now, I'd like to invite anyone who wants to ask Christ into their hearts to come forward."

Our pastor does this at every service, and there are two mentally disabled men who always go to the altar at the foot of the stage, get on their knees, and pray with the church staff. Once in a while, there are one or two more.

Tonight, over 20 people race to the front, the most I've ever seen. Then some slower stragglers, dabbing at runny roses and wet cheeks, follow. The worship band takes the stage and plays soft, acoustic music as the church staff prays with the soon-to-be-believers.

"Ooooh shalalalakananaoki, ooooh shalalalakananaoki, kananananashanani…" a woman exclaims, now standing with her hands raised toward heaven, on the main floor of the church.

Mom closes her eyes and lifts her hands skyward.

Speaking in tongues, one of the gifts of the Spirit, is when you speak gibberish to God, but He understands you. They say people have been known to speak in tongues in a language they don't normally know, like Italian or Swahili. Sometimes people do it quietly to themselves, and sometimes they pull focus during a service. When that happens, it's God talking to us through the person, and there is often an interpretation in English through someone else in the congregation that follows.

Seems like we could just cut to the interpretation, but what do I know?

"Shalalalaakanananana oh my ooooh shananananana oh my oooooh shananananananana..."

The woman continues while everything else stops: the worship band puts down their instruments, the people who were exiting freeze, and the staff praying with the new believers divert their attention to her. Everyone holds their breath with anticipation about what this word from God will be: a prophecy? An encouragement? An admonishment?

It'll probably be the usual: God loves us, trust in Him, something like that.

I wonder why I've never spoken in tongues or delivered an interpretation. Am I not close enough to God? Am I dead inside?

Even though it's a holy gift of the Spirit, a girl in school made me laugh when she made fun of speaking in tongues by closing her eyes, raising her hands, and shouting, "shouldaboughtahondabutiboughtahyundai!"

The woman stops speaking in tongues and collapses into the pew like a rag doll.

"And now we will wait for the interpretation," our pastor says solemnly.

A man stands up on the other side of the church.

Here we go.

"My children! This is the Lord speaking. I want you to know that I love you, my children. You have been set apart for my work. Cast your cares upon me and trust me, my children..."

Called it.

When the interpretation finishes, the pastor thanks God for this word and dismisses the service. The people at the foot of the stage who just accepted Christ are given Bibles and information about the church.

Mom, on cloud nine, collects her purse and stands up.

"God is using this show in a mighty way. That was incredible," she says.

But something doesn't feel right to me.

Should people be scared into becoming Christians? Shouldn't God's love compel them?

Last Sunday, our pastor showed a trailer for the show to spark excitement, and the last shot was of a seven-year-old kid being interviewed after the show.

"Why did you accept Jesus into your heart tonight?" the interviewer asks.

"Because I don't want to go to Hell!" the boy says, his eyes wide with fear.

Just as we start to leave our seats, a tall, blonde woman taps my shoulder gently, and I turn around.

Oh, no.

It's common at our church for someone to pull you aside and deliver a personal message from God, and I hate it. I'm always afraid God is going to tell someone something embarrassing or bad that I did, like how recently I've started looking up certain words in the dictionary alone that give me this really hot feeling (lust, sex, libido…).

If she tells me she knows about that, I WILL DIE.

"God put it on my heart to ask you if you're worried about something that I can pray for?" the woman says sweetly.

Well, I was worried God told you something about me, and now you're telling me God told you something about me!

CHAPTER 7

FOR REAL THIS TIME, ARMAGEDDON ON THE FLAT EARTH

"IF WHAT A PROPHET proclaims in the name of the Lord does not take place or come true, that is a message the Lord has not spoken."

-Deuteronomy 18:22

~14~

I'm sitting at the piano in the living room, going over a tricky second soprano harmony for varsity choir while *Dick Clark's New Year's Rockin' Eve* plays muted on the TV. Now that I'm a freshman in high school, I can stay up late sometimes, especially when it's the end of the world.

"I suppose we can still bang the pots and pans," Mom says cheerfully, as she searches cupboards in the kitchen for musical utensils. Apparently, it's an old tradition to hit the streets at midnight on New Year's Eve and clang cookware to celebrate the new year.

She's in a great mood, because even though Y2K (the year 2000) is upon us and society is supposedly going to collapse because nothing was made to work beyond years that start with 19, she thinks this is the kickoff of those sweet, sweet End Times.

The Antichrist will soon seize power in the wake of this technology-induced chaos.

"Sure, Mom."

I've held in eye rolls as much as I could, but over the last few months, some have slipped out as she's gone overboard stockpiling supplies. One wall of our garage is a pantry now with cans of beans, vegetables, and soup, bags of pasta and rice, and jars of jams and sauces. Another garage wall holds jugs of gasoline. Then there are the buckets of gold and silver coins hidden in my parents' closet since U.S. Dollars will supposedly be worthless.

My eyes glance from the two white barrels for catching rainwater in the backyard (it rained recently, but Mom forgot to remove the lids) to the dining room table where Mom is proudly surveying a mound of flashlights and battery-operated radios.

Hm, is my mother an extremist?

People in our church are concerned about Y2K, too, but no one has gone to the lengths Dawn Huckle has. Dad is wary of what's going to happen at midnight, but it's past his bedtime.

Some numbers potentially glitching in devices mean there won't be food or water for months? Seems like a stretch. After all, Dad isn't healed yet, and in all my 14 years, the Rapture has always been "just around the corner."

I can confidently say I've witnessed one miracle, though: when my begging somehow convinced my parents to let me attend the public (godless! worldly! dangerous!) high school in town known for its exceptional choir and drama programs (as well as light gang and drug activity).

In my pitch, I reminded them how imperfect even my sheltered Christian junior high was. There was the time my math teacher told the class that she had recently discovered pornographic VHSs in her home, and now, her husband was addressing his porn addiction through prayer and counseling from the church. Mom hit the roof over the inappropriate subject matter, and I was creeped out thinking about this side of a man we saw in church every Sunday.

While my parents were fearful of the leap from my tiny, religious junior high to a public high school with over 2,000 students, I've never been more at home than around my newfound choir and drama nerds. The musical revue we did the summer before my freshman year was the most fun I've ever had. We all yell "Nakey time!" when changing in the dressing room. It's the best!

My secular schoolmates and their families are concerned about Y2K but not in a fulfillment-of-the-prophecy kind of way.

Rumor is I'm being considered for a coveted soprano spot that will be open next year in the elite Madrigal choir. If the world doesn't end tonight, that is.

"It's almost midnight!" Mom squeals.

She plops on the couch, armed with a battery-powered radio in one hand and a flashlight in the other, and unmutes the TV. I turn around on the piano bench to face the TV, and we watch the ball descend in New York City.

"5! 4! 3!"

We hold our breath for the big moment.

Could this really be it?

"2!"

Mom braces herself: shoulders up, mouth open, flashlight raised.

"1! Happy 2000!" Dick Clark says.

The show, and our electricity, continue without a hitch.

Sorry, Mom, no apocalypse.

"Huh, I guess they fixed it in time," she says, looking around for signs of breakdown, unfazed that her preparations were in vain. She must have felt that she'd rather be ready for disaster and look foolish if it doesn't happen than ever be unprepared.

Maybe that's why she became a Christian in the first place?

I watch her go to the kitchen, grab a silver pot and wooden spoon, and head to the front yard to usher in what has turned out to be a run-of-the-mill New Year's Eve. I keep in a snotty "I told you so," grab a pot and soup ladle, and join her outside in the chilly California winter night.

"Happy New Year! Whoo-hoo!" we both shout, laughing at ourselves while we bang cookware on our otherwise quiet residential street.

Add Y2K to the list of false alarms for the End Times.

CHAPTER 8
EAT, PRAY, FLAT EARTH

"...URGE the younger women to love their husbands and children, to be self-controlled and pure, to be busy at home, to be kind, and to be subject to their husbands..."
  -Titus 2:4-5

~16~

I've been dreading this call, but now I have to make it, or I'll explode. The knots in my stomach are thrashing and twisting, but at least I have notecards.

In my red and white Christmas pajamas, my long, straight hair in a messy slept-in pony, I pick up our landline phone in the den (the middle of the house for all to hear, UGH), take a deep breath, and dial my sort-of-boyfriend's number. I look out the window at the gray sky. Crummy, crummy, crummy.

Ring. Heartbeat.

Ring. Heartbeat, heartbeat.

Ring. Heartbeat, heartbeat, heartbeat.

"Hello?" says Matt's younger brother Luke.

"Hi, Luke, is Matt there? This is Susan." I'm trying to sound super normal, but probably overdoing it.

"Hi, Susan!" He sounds delighted to hear my voice.

Ugh.

"Yeah, let me get him!"

Heartbeat, heartbeat, HEARTBEAT!

I'm as uncomfortable now as I was at our first date at In-N-Out, where our moms dropped us off for lunch a month ago. A 16-year-old (me), a 17-year-old (him), and two Double-Doubles, what could go wrong? I tried to make him laugh and carry on a normal conversation, but I just felt kill-me awkward.

People told me he liked me, and he seemed to light up whenever we'd see each other at school. So, to make him and everyone else happy, I said yes over AIM (AOL Instant Messenger) to being his girlfriend, whatever that actually means.

Since then, our dating has consisted of talking on the phone and chatting on AIM. We haven't even kissed. He's tall with dirty blonde hair in the style of Jonathan Taylor Thomas, but his acne-ridden face is not inviting. He's a Christian, a talented musician and composer, and he likes me. *Maybe that's enough*, I'd thought.

NOPE. I don't feel the same way he does, and I can't pretend anymore. But I hate hurting someone's feelings. This is going to suuuuuuuuuck.

"Hey, sweetheart!" Matt says brightly into the phone.

I cringe. My toes curl.

"How are you?" he continues.

He sounds so happy. Now would be a GREAT time for the Rapture.

"Hi, Matt," I say, my pitch falling.

I look down at the index cards in my hand that have the points I'd like to make in delicate, strategic wording. I don't trust myself to say everything just right if I wing it. Pretending I'm a lawyer who needs to persuade a jury with logical arguments helps take the emotion out of it.

"I think we shouldn't date anymore because-"

"What?" he says, flabbergasted. I can't blame him. I've played the part of enthusiastic girlfriend very well.

Panic scrambles my brain and blurs my vision, so I cut to the end of my notes.

"I…I think it would be better if we were just friends."

Relief.

Silence.

"Susan, that is not God's plan for us."

"Hm?"

"God has given me visions of our future together: we are leading worship at this church in Oregon in ten years. I'm playing piano, and you're singing. I've seen how it's supposed to be. God showed me."

Why didn't God show me?

He sounds so serious, and that's who he is: a very serious person. Serious about music, serious about God, serious about being serious.

Boring!

Also, I want to be an actor, not lead worship at a church in Oregon. That sounds unbearably uninteresting (sorry, God). I don't know if he's just saying this to keep me from breaking up with him or if he really had visions, but I know that I can't feel this uncomfortable with dating him if it's God's will.

"I guess…I guess I don't see that for me," I stammer. "I'm really, really sorry, Matt."

"Uh, okay. Huh. Wow. I just…"

His words fade into a quiet whimper, and I'm no help. My mouth hangs open and twitches softly as I search for the magic words that will make it all better.

I got nothing.

Eventually, we mumble goodbyes and hang up awkwardly. That's when I have a scandalous thought.

Now that we're broken up, I can call him my 'ex.'

The delicious raciness of that term makes my imagination run wild with all the ways I can drop such a mature word in casual conversation.

I go to the kitchen and hold the pantry door open, half looking to eat my feelings, half lost in thought about dating, God's will, Oregon, sex-

"What's the matter?" Mom says.

I realize she's been washing the dishes behind me while I've been staring into the pantry in a daze.

"I just broke up with Matt," I say weakly, my eyes transfixed on a box of Hi-C juice boxes. My heart rate is back to normal, but the stomach knots are still there.

"Oh. Well, 'tis the season!" she says, like this is the expression you always say at a time like this. "It's almost Christmas, it's winter. Relationships end or begin around now."

Is love seasonal?

Like most everything before she became a Christian, she's tight-lipped about her dating history. We are both mortified to talk about this aspect of life with each other, but she's dropped a few tips before this one.

Once, while I was basking in the romantic ending of *The Mirror Has Two Faces*, when my idol Barbra Streisand and Jeff Bridges dance in the streets together, Mom marched into the living room with her yellow rubber gloves dripping with soapy water and stopped the VHS with a yank of her elbow.

"You know, love isn't really like that, Susan," she said, pursing her lips and shaking her head. "Stuff like that doesn't happen in real life."

Jeez, Mom, can't a girl dream?

We were at a restaurant once when we both noticed a strikingly beautiful, tall, thin woman in skin-tight floral capri pants walk by.

"She is asking for trouble," Mom muttered into her soup. "Don't ever dress like that, Susan." I've been covered in baggy clothes, neck to ankles, ever since.

I've picked up other dating-related information in school. In health class, I got an eye-opening dose of the male anatomy and

an eye-closing dose of what sexually transmitted diseases look like.

I've overheard people at school talk about how a guy's thing grows during sex, and I must be deformed because there is absolutely NO WAY that anything of that size could fit in whatever I have *down there*. It goes without saying that I can't have sex until I'm married because pre-marital sex is a sin, but it's also to protect my heart. All guys want is sex, apparently, and once they get it, they drop you like a hot potato unless they can't because you're married.

"Each time you have sex with a new person, you give a piece of your heart away," our youth pastor says. "You want to have something left to give your husband, right?"

Since sex/marriage is a long way away, I'm not going to worry about this for as long as possible. To stay pure, I dare not explore whatever is *down there*.

Luckily, there are no guys my age that I'm even remotely attracted to, so it's easy to follow God's law of abstinence. It was fun stage kissing Joe, who played my husband when I was the lead in *Dial 'M' for Murder* at school, but he's like all my male peers: skinny, bony, awkward, and immature.

My girlfriends tell me about their crushes on a guy in choir or French:

"Austin has the best voice!"

"Jared's eyes are heaven!"

And all I can think is *Ugh, boys*. I want a Man: broad-chested, smart, world-wise. I don't care about Austin's voice or Jared's eyes. I want my teachers. And I want them bad.

First, it was my geometry teacher, Mr. Stone. It wasn't his aging surfer look: short blonde hair with a few coifed waves in front contrasted by a dark red tan. It wasn't his clothes: puffy khakis and old polos. It was his offbeat sense of humor and how pleased he was with my proofs.

Then it was Mr. Phillips who taught sophomore English. When he said one day in class that he used to live in Los Angeles until all his writer friends committed suicide, I wanted to hold him forever. When I gave extended answers to a question in class, he wore his thoughtful, curious listening face, and I basked in the attention from someone so smart.

Do I just like the male teachers who seem to like me?

I observed my fellow females in Mr. Gonzalez's freshman English class perfect the art of leaning over a teacher's desk in a tight, low-cut shirt while asking an earnest-seeming question. His claim to fame was that he had played golf against Tiger Woods once, but he was fresh out of college, so I wasn't interested. Too young.

These days, if I didn't have the fear of God in me about pre-marital sex, I would be throwing myself at Mr. Smith, my econ teacher (what is it about men who are good with numbers?). He is tall with dark hair, in his 30s, and not sexy by traditional standards, but everything about him says *experienced*. He's recently divorced and has two small children. It's devastatingly hot to think about soothing him while he bravely soldiers on for the sake of his kids. He has a lisp, so teaching about thupply and demand does him no favors, but the heart wants what it wants.

"And what do we call it when there'th more of a good than there ith demand?" Mr. Smith asks the class while tapping out a graph on the board, his back to us.

My hormone-filled blood pumps in my veins while the classroom's fluorescent lights hum. I raise my hand, hoping no armpit sweat is visible. He turns around to face the few hands that are raised. His dark, sad eyes behind black curls lock with mine.

"Susan?"

He says the 's's perfectly. My name on his lips feels like taking a bath in chocolate. I lower my hand and part my lips.

"Surplus?" I say, coyly, crossing my legs in loose faded jeans.

"Thath's right," he says, holding my gaze an extra beat. He turns back to the board and starts tapping out a new graph. I watch the semi-muscles in his arms vibrate with the movement.

As long as the only men I'm interested in are off-limits adults, God's got nothing to worry about.

Postscript

In the year after our break-up, Matt released a CD of original music dedicated to me.

He ended up in Oregon.

CHAPTER 9
SERIOUSLY, THIS IS IT NOW, END TIMES ON THE FLAT EARTH

"FOR I KNOW the plans I have for you…plans to give you hope and a future."
-Jeremiah 29:11

~17~

"So, how's school going?" Dad asks over breakfast at Jack's, a country diner near our home.

I have something big to announce, but I'm nervous to open with it, so I push around my biscuit crumbles swimming in a bowl of gravy.

Dad started this monthly father-daughter breakfast tradition during my junior year, and it's a sweet attempt of his to connect.

Or does he just like breakfast at Jack's?

Parenting seems easier for him now that he can talk to me like an adult. He looks like Jerry Seinfeld, and I take after him: big forehead, straight hair, and big lips, which is why Don in French greets me with, "La bouche!" (the mouth).

Unfazed that I haven't answered yet, Dad dives into his egg white omelet. He inhales meals like there's a time limit, something apparently drilled into him in the Air Force.

"Well, AP Stats is pretty easy so far. I like this new medley we're doing in Madrigals. Our AP Government teacher memorized all our names on the first day, that was pretty impressive-"

"Susan, the banks are on the verge of collapse," he says in a hushed tone, his lips and face tight. His dark blue eyes dart around to see if anyone is listening. He looks pained, and his thin frame is as stiff as his white, collared shirt.

That's enough about school, I guess.

"We probably have about 16-24 months before they do. I need you to be prepared for what's to come."

"Welcome to Jack's! Where'd y'all like to sit?" The server's cheery greeting from the front of the restaurant cuts through our tense conversation. We like this place because it's easy for Dad to navigate with his cane. By now, all the adjustments for his paralysis are second nature: vetting restaurants for accessibility, a wheelchair always in the trunk just in case, grab bars, and a shower seat in the bathroom.

"You should always invest in gold because cash will soon be worthless. Don't panic when there's a run on the banks. We have what we need." He picks his fork back up and mutters into his plate, "We should never have gone off the gold standard in the '70s."

With a bachelor's degree in economics and how closely he follows financial markets, he must know what he's talking about, right?

He seems incredibly knowledgeable about the one-world government coming, the corruption of the Federal Reserve and American government, and the instability of the banks. He also says "fiat currency" a lot, which sounds important. I'm onto Mom's penchant for extremism, but he's more educated than she and logical, so I give his words more weight. I'm not sure what exactly I'm supposed to do, though, in the event of the banks collapsing.

Can I still be an actor? That's all I care about.

"Dad, I think God told me where I'm supposed to go to college," I say after a long pause.

"Oh?" He stops eating, puts his fork down, and looks at me. I don't often have his full attention.

"I was flipping through a big book of colleges yesterday during study hall and found a section that lists all the ones that have theatre degrees. When my eyes landed on 'The University of North Carolina at Chapel Hill,' I felt like God was telling me this is where I'm supposed to go. I was sort of struck by the words and couldn't move my eyes from the name, even though I've never heard of it."

This feeling came over me that I'm guessing is what people feel when God is telling them something. I've been looking for some direction about where to go, and that feeling seemed good enough.

"They have a great journalism and mass communication department, too," I add. That can be my practical degree for my parents while I double major in theatre for me. It also doesn't hurt that Chapel Hill is very, very, very far away from my small, boring California town.

Whew! It's out!

"Oh," he says, taking this in slowly and thoughtfully, as he does with everything. It's why I want to be exactly like him and nothing like Mom, with one exception.

Last year, to our surprise, Dad wanted to see the movie *A Beautiful Mind,* because it's about someone he admires: John Nash, the brilliant, schizophrenic mathematician. Dad was so overwhelmed by the intensity of the story and the movie theatre experience (he hadn't been in ages) that he vomited on the way home.

"Okay," he finally says to my college choice. He can't argue with God's plan, so he resumes inhaling his meal.

Mom can't say no with Dad and God on my side.

———

Months later, I open the letter I've been waiting for from the University of North Carolina at Chapel Hill. The words sting like a bucket of freezing water to the face.

Too bad God forgot to tell them to accept me!

I re-read the letter, thinking I must be misunderstanding.

Really, God? I trusted you! Was that not you?

I knew it'd be hard to get in as an out-of-state student, but my GPA is 4.3! My SAT score is above average!

My face sags from all the egg on it as I take slow bites of an atrocious casserole at dinner later that week. It's Dad's favorite: crunchy sausage, limp noodles, and watery tomato sauce.

Bleck.

I fill my plate with rolls and salad and just a bit of the casserole, most of which I'll cover with my napkin and trash. I'm trying to embrace my backup plan (*or is THIS your will, God?*): attend North Carolina State University (*they* accepted me), and then transfer to Chapel Hill for my sophomore year since it'll be easier to get in as a transfer student.

"How was school today?" Mom asks, taking a heaping bite of Hell's casserole.

"Fine," I whine.

I made a fool of myself in chemistry today, but I'll keep that to myself. Mr. Hughes was trying to think of the country that starts with a 'g' that related to the experiment we were doing, and while everyone was shouting ideas ("Germany?" "Greece?" "Ghana, Mr. H?"), I confidently contributed my guess:

"Gonads?"

Just as the word left my mouth, I felt how wrong it was. Muffled giggles throughout the classroom slowly turned into loud, uncontrollable guffaws as I sank into my chair, red-faced.

"Should we tell her?" Mom says quietly to Dad, as if I'm not there.

I look up at them, and they are grinning ear to ear: Mom with her perfect teeth outlined by bright pink lipstick and Dad with his closed-mouth grin, masking the crowded teeth he's embarrassed of. Maybe it's the light reflecting off their glasses, but their eyes look like they're dancing. I want to slap them.

"Daddy is going to retire at the end of May," she says.

Well, he is 60, so I guess that makes sense.

"Cool," I mumble. I can't cover the casserole with my napkin yet because they're still looking right at me.

"And we're going to move this summer to North Carolina. We can all live together in Raleigh while you do your freshman year at N.C. State," she says.

WHAT?

It never occurred to me that they would leave California.

"You don't want to be in the dorms, Susan," she adds with a shudder. "They're hotbeds of sin."

"Oh," I get out after too long.

The white marble angel over the doorway to the kitchen (there's one on almost every wall) catches my eye.

Is that a smirk?

"You thought you were getting away from your parents! Hahahahaha!" the angel's expression seems to say.

I guess this is all part of God's plan?

CHAPTER 10
FLAT EARTH VS. ROUND

"...YOU must not associate with anyone who...is sexually immoral or greedy, an idolator or slanderer, a drunkard or swindler. Do not even eat with such people."

-1 Corinthians 5:11

~18~

We rarely see my aunt and uncle since they live in another country (Northern California), but they've come down to have a farewell dinner with us before we move to North Carolina the week after I graduate high school. We're doing a four-day cross-country drive instead of a four-and-a-half-hour flight cause Mom won't fly post-9/11.

My parents always speak of Mom's older brother and his wife as lost, worldly people. They're Democrats, divorcees, and atheists, so I find them fascinating.

I keep adjusting my flowy, pink dress as we wait for them to join us at the restaurant, pecking like a chicken at the loose shoulder straps from my lack of boobs and stretched fabric around my thunder thighs. If I had popcorn, I'd be nervously munching handfuls in anticipation of the show: the careful dinner conversation of two couples who couldn't be more different but somehow are family.

"I'm sure they'll be drunk by the end of dinner," Mom whispers to Dad, her bold, chunky jewelry popping against the backdrop of her navy turtleneck.

Dad fidgets with the splint that holds his paralyzed left forearm in place, and I notice how skinny that arm is now. Mom taps her acrylic nails on the table. We're meeting my aunt and uncle where they're staying: the historic Santa Maria Inn, shiny chestnut wood everywhere under dim, warm lighting. This way, they can stumble to their rooms after dinner.

"John! Dawn! Susan! Good to see you all!" Uncle Dave bellows as he approaches our table. He has bright white hair around a bald spot that shines under the lights, and I remember how warm he is. A big, easy smile never leaves his face.

"Susan, look at you!" Aunt Liz says, in her nasal tone. She's a sexy, stylish flight attendant who talks out of one side of her mouth and always wears something exotic from her travels that will cue a story. Tonight, my money's on the green and blue silk scarf around her neck.

Uncle Dave gives me a bear hug, and Aunt Liz offers a delicate embrace before we take our seats, and the server approaches. My parents aren't huggy with each other or me, so things are already off to a wacky start with the heathens.

"We'll do a bottle of your Paso cab," my uncle says to the server with a wink. My aunt gives him a girlish smile about the wine choice and rubs his arm with approval.

They're touching each other AND drinking!

"Melissa, is it?" Dad says, squinting to read the server's name tag. "Melissa, Melissa," he says under his breath, trying to memorize it.

Why does he always do this?

God forbid it's an unusual name, and my parents never shut up about it ("Rina? Riana what? Ri-an-non, oh, Rhiannon! Now, where does *that* name come from?").

"Four wine glasses?" Melissa asks.

"None for us. Just water, thanks," Mom says, not hiding her judgment. "Oh, remember when you used to get Shirley Temples here, Susan? Want one of those?"

"Water's fine," I say.

Honestly, a Shirley Temple sounds great, but I'm not a kid anymore.

"So, how's retirement going, Dave?" Mom asks, characteristically taking charge of the conversation.

"Oh, Dawn, you just know he'd never give up working on Porsches," Liz says, with a smirk.

"Well, yeah, I can't help myself, I guess. People from all over the world keep sending me engines to fix."

He was an engineer, and when I was little, he'd always draw me a perfect car on scratch paper while we were out to eat. He even wrote a book about Porsches. Mom and Grandma always roll their eyes about this book, fixating on the numerous girl-friends he mentions and how un-Christian flashy cars are. I thought the book was impressive.

"How about you, John? What are you going to do after you retire?" my uncle asks.

"Oh, I don't know," Dad says quietly. He doesn't like being the center of attention. "I'm looking forward to spending more time in the Word."

My aunt and uncle exchange glances, then light up when they see that the wine is on its way.

"Can you guess where this neckerchief is from?" Aunt Liz says, after Melissa leaves with our meal orders. Before anyone can reply, she says in her Mae West cadence, "A sheik proposed to me once on a layover, and when I turned him down, he gave me this to remember him by. So, you better stay on your toes, Dave!" She lets out a nasal cackle while my imagination runs wild, envisioning her globe-trotting life.

Last summer, Mom discouraged me from going on my high

school's choir trip to Europe. "You won't like it, Susan. You're a homebody," she said.

Am I?

"You won't be flying to Iraq anytime soon, I hope," Dad says to Liz.

"This invasion is just…nonsense," she replies, apparently stopping herself from saying more.

"Well, we have to do something after what they did to us on 9/11," Mom says, her eyes fiery.

Dad jumps in. "Rush says-"

"Rush?" Dave says, incredulously. "Oh, John, you don't listen to him, do you?"

Dad looks flabbergasted by this reaction to Rush Limbaugh. Liz hiccups.

"Of course, we do!" Mom says.

Dave and Liz sigh. Dad jumps back in.

"Weapons of mass destruction are-"

"Food's here!" says Dave.

Mercifully, our meals take over the conversation ("Oo, this smells good!" "Well, look at that!" "Thank you, *Melissa*!"). When Dave and Liz launch into a routine about their last big party (The drinks! The games! The laughs!), I realize my parents don't even host Bible study anymore because it stresses Mom out to have people over.

Dave and Liz grow increasingly jubilant as the wine disappears, while my parents stay painfully sober.

"So, Susan, will you be getting your M. R. S. degree in college?" Aunt Liz asks with purple teeth, giggling. My uncle snorts, and my parents brace themselves.

"Huh? Oh. Just a double major in journalism and theatre, I think," I say, squashing that topic, shuddering at the memory of my breakup with Matt, my one pathetic dating experience, if you could even call it that.

"Oh? Well, there's time. We met our husbands later in life, didn't we, Dawn?" Liz says, giving Dave another arm squeeze.

"Second wives are best!" Uncle Dave says, laughing and toasting Liz with wine from their second bottle. They all rehash my uncle's first wife debacle: Val, notorious, Italian Val, who filed for divorce after she got what she wanted out of the marriage, apparently: two babies and some alimony. I bet there's more to the story, but that's how it's been distilled over the years. I have three cousins total, and I've never met the two from this marriage because Val kept the kids away from Dave post-divorce.

"'He who finds a wife finds a good thing and obtains favor from the Lord.' Proverbs 18:22," Dad says with a smile. My aunt and uncle gulp their wine.

"Good one, John," my uncle says when he comes up for air.

"'House and wealth are inherited from fathers, but a prudent wife is from the Lord.' Proverbs 19:14," Dad adds with a gleam in his eye.

"Oh, there's another one!" Aunt Liz says. "You lucked out, Dawn," she mutters into her wine glass.

"Are you kidding me? I knew as soon as we met," Mom says, looking at Dad adoringly. A younger woman's smile comes over her when she talks about meeting my dad. "I mean, a lawyer? With blue eyes? Just what I wanted!" she squeals.

"You wouldn't marry someone who didn't have blue eyes?" I ask in disbelief at such shallow criteria.

"Absolutely not!" she laughs. Dad blushes and then starts laughing at what he's about to say, so much so that he can barely get it out. Dad loves his own jokes best.

"She got a husband-" He fights through his laughter to finish his sentence, his voice getting higher and higher. "-and I got her credit card debt!" They all howl, but I've heard this line a million times.

It's hard for me to imagine my conservative, cautious parents getting married in early March 1979, mere months after meeting at a mutual friend's Thanksgiving party in Santa Barbara. When they met, they were delighted to discover that they were both 36, single, from small towns in New York, and had recently become born-again Christians. Whether you believe in destiny or not, it's hard to dismiss that they seemed cosmically set up. Mom's dyed blonde hair didn't hurt either, Dad's favorite.

At the end of the evening, as we all get up to go, Aunt Liz pulls me aside. The unfamiliar smells of wine and her exotic perfume catch my breath.

"Look, I know your parents are pretty loony, so if you ever need to talk to a normal person, call me," she says, out of one side of her mouth, her eyes glassy and unfocused.

The dance I've been doing all night, between loyalty to my parents and curiosity about my aunt and uncle, comes to an abrupt end.

Do I roll my eyes along with her and nod in agreement, or do I stand by my devout parents?

"Oh. Thank you, but I'm okay," I mumble.

You must be the loony one for not being a Christian, Aunt Liz.

After four days of driving across the country with my parents, with daily stops at Cracker Barrel and hourly shrieks of "Slow down, Susan!" we whiz by the Welcome to North Carolina sign on I-40. When I was little, we did a cross-country road trip to Tennessee to scope out the area because Dad had a job offer there. Mom said, "Too many trees," and we turned around. She has the same sour look on her face now.

Four hours later, we stop for lunch at a Quizno's less than an hour away from the apartment in Raleigh that we're going to share for my freshman year of college at N.C. State. The three of us are walking across the parking lot in a road-weary daze when a sandy-haired middle-aged woman in a dowdy housedress stops us.

"Is that your father out there?" she says to Mom in her syrupy southern drawl.

Mom looks at her, puzzled. Her father died before I was born, and it seems pretty clear we aren't with anyone else. The woman repeats her question and points across the parking lot to no one. We stare at her, not knowing what to say.

It finally registers that she's pointing to a car with its lights on, and with clearer, slower enunciation, she says, "Is that your Volvo out there?"

"Oh! Volvo!" Mom says. We laugh at this Southern accent-induced miscommunication over lunch and all the way to Raleigh.

Oh, boy, is this how it's going to be?

Postscript

That dinner turned out to be the last time I saw my uncle, who passed away seven years later. My parents cut him and my aunt out of their lives after a catch-up phone call turned into a screaming match. Mom was begging Dave to accept Christ or be doomed to Hell, and he was demanding she drop it once and for all.

They'd always been kind to me, so I never stopped sending them Christmas cards.

CHAPTER 11
U. OF F.E., PART 1

"HONOR YOUR FATHER AND MOTHER."
-Ephesians 6:2

~18~

Yesterday, I was basking in the glow of my stellar first semester grades, thinking how ridiculous all my high school teachers were for hyping up hard, scary college when Mom dropped a bomb.

"I'm leaving you and your father," she said, numb, resigned, and pale from head to toe in her white robe and unkept, short blonde hair. She used to have dark roots, now they're white.

"I'm completely exhausted. I cannot take care of you or your father anymore. I want to start a new life." Her cool blue eyes stayed lost in the marble countertop of the breakfast bar between us. I stopped what I was doing in the kitchen to focus on her and listen, but that was it. She turned and floated back to her room. I didn't see Dad all day. I emailed my high school best friend, Lauren, about it and asked her to pray for my mom.

Now I'm rage collaging. My normally Type-A, neat, and organized bedroom looks like Michaels exploded as I tape photos and programs haphazardly into this brown scrapbook. I've been making scrapbooks since high school, saving every theatre ticket, show program, and photo that makes me feel like my life is going somewhere.

What have I done? Why does she need to leave me? I'm a self-sufficient college student who isn't living with my parents by choice, so why am I lumped in with Dad's affliction as a burden to her? Most parents would be thrilled to have a straight-A, church-going kid who's never had sex, snuck out, cussed, done drugs, smoked, or consumed alcohol! Where's my Daughter of the Year award?

Instead, she chides me when I express a different opinion once in a while. "You just love to argue," she snips, and nothing makes me want to argue more.

In fairness, I've probably been too absorbed in my college life of classes, homework, rehearsals, and new friends to notice how depressed she's been since we moved here. I've tried my whole life to ignore how high and low she can run, focusing instead on staying out of her way. We never talk about the antidepressants she's on, but I know she's been on them for years because Dad let it slip once how helpful her pills are for his insomnia.

I slap a photo of me playing the queen in a college Madrigal dinner theatre show into my scrapbook when my stomach gurgles with hunger. Time to leave my room and face whatever the update is.

Has she left already? Where did she go? Will I have to take care of Dad by myself?

As I gingerly approach the kitchen, I'm shocked to see Mom fully put together with makeup on, hair coiffed, bright colors donned, flitting about, whipping something up for lunch.

"Should we drive around and look at Christmas lights tonight?" she says, all smiles.

Now I'm really angry. While I silently process this 180, I grab some bread off the counter to make toast.

"Or we can watch *White Christmas*, your favorite," she says, heaping gobs of cream cheese on bread.

"Are we just going to pretend you didn't say you're leaving us yesterday?" I retort so aggressively that I slam the toaster door shut and twist the knob to the darkest setting.

I feel like a fool for taking yesterday's declaration seriously!

She looks at me sheepishly and takes a long pause.

"I feel better today," she says quietly, then shifts her mood back into high gear. "So, let's go look at Christmas lights tonight!" With that, she takes her plate, sits on the couch, and turns on HGTV.

How dare she play with my heart like this! I have to keep everything inside for fear of ever upsetting her, but she gets unlimited outbursts she can takesies-backsies?

Smoke comes out of my ears and the toaster oven.

~19~

It's almost 6 am, and I'm driving home from a party in a fog of drowsiness and heartbreak. My theatre friends and I planned the evening to celebrate the end of finals and our freshman year, but we ended up watching all *The Lord of the Rings* movies to distract me from being let down gently by the first guy I ever liked (who wasn't an off-limits teacher).

With his long, dark hair, tall frame, and senior's maturity, I'd been smitten with Michael ever since he handed me a whiskey at my first theatre party. I only took one awful sip of it while he sat behind me and rubbed my shoulders. We went on a few dates, and I fell hard and fast. I foolishly stayed up late and signed into AIM just in case he signed on, and if he did, even more foolishly waited for him to write me first.

When he told me he couldn't get involved because he was off to law school next year, I played it off ("Of course! No worries! I get it!") then promptly vomited. I guess it runs in the family.

Our romantic and painful moments keep swirling in my head, interrupted by random flashes of *The Lord of the Rings* scenes, as I pull up to my parents' apartment.

Is that a cop car parked in front?
Did something happen to them?
Oh, no.
Is this about me coming home so late?

My phone's battery died late last night, before I knew this would turn into an all-nighter, so I didn't call them. I figured Dad gets up at 6:30 am at the earliest, so I'd be fine as long as I was home before then. I often come home from a rehearsal after they've gone to bed.

I push through my sleepy haze and hurriedly park and get to the front door. The moment I enter, all the faces inside, my parents' and a cop's, relax at once.

"Oh, thank God," Mom exhales, falling into a seat at the kitchen table.

"Your parents were very worried about you," the handsome, young cop says, closing his notepad. I feel a strange mix of shame and attraction. "Well, my work here is done," he sighs. He gives me a stern look as he walks past me and leaves.

"I'm so sorry," I sputter, shutting the door. "I was with Brandy, Josh, Curt, and Khoa, and we were watching movies…" I trail off, knowing what I'm saying isn't helping.

Mom takes a deep breath, her nostrils now flaring.

"You were so down, I thought you did something stupid," she spits. "You scared me half to death. Don't you ever do that again," she says, pointing at me, then heading to her room to collapse.

Seated at the kitchen table in his navy pajamas, Dad looks at me with an indecipherable look, his eyes sunken in from the lack of sleep, his hair grayer than I remember. He probably didn't appreciate me coming home so late without notice, but I think he gets that I am an adult now.

I go to my room with my tail between my legs, crawl into bed, and plug my phone in to charge next to me. I regret worrying them, but I'm 19. I don't think that what I did was wrong.

Just as the cocktail of emotions is about to put me into a deep but not so sound sleep, my phone buzzes with a voicemail from last night. I hit 'Play.'

"Susan, it's Mom. PLEASE, call us, PLEASE!" Mom's voice shakes, and I instantly picture her crying and trembling. It shatters my heart into a million pieces, so I delete it before listening to the rest.

I think it's time to not live with my parents anymore.

I hold the covers over my cold nose as my eyes catch the letter pinned to my corkboard from UNC-Chapel Hill declaring my acceptance as a transfer student for the fall of my sophomore year. Because my parents have lived in the state for a year, I'll have significantly cheaper in-state tuition for my last three years of college there.

The Lord works in mysterious ways.

CHAPTER 12
U. OF F.E., PART 2

"AND SO THESE men of Indostan
  Disputed loud and long,
  Each in his own opinion
  Exceeding stiff and strong,
  Though each was partly in the right,
  And all were in the wrong!"
-John Godfrey Saxe

~21~

It's my 21st birthday, and I'm pounding water at Cheesecake Factory with my parents and my boyfriend, Keith. I'm tipsy on validation because I've been hired for my first paid acting job: a lead role in *The Last Night of Ballyhoo* at a local regional theatre for the summer that pays $1000 a week! Why would anyone do anything else?

Unsure how to dress for a milestone birthday but also Cheesecake Factory, I landed on nice jeans that are long enough to flare around my tan heels, a sheer pale pink top with flowers at the bottom, and a not-so-sheer top underneath for my parents' sake.

Conversation in our cramped booth, Keith and I on one side, my parents on the other, is a light-hearted game of us vs. them, sometimes young people vs. old, but mostly it's Californians vs. rural Carolina-born and bred Keith. Luckily, we're all Christians.

"Y'all've never had deep-fried Oreos at the state fair?" Keith twangs in his dark green corduroy button-down shirt, sipping his sweet tea.

"We've never been to a state fair!" Mom laughs, downing her Arnold Palmer.

Thank God they get along.

Keith is a sandy-haired, tan southern gentleman who knows how to talk to parents. We met through the theatre department at N.C. State, and he became my boyfriend in my sophomore year after a hot and heavy clothes-on summer. Mom emailed me, "We do not approve of an unmarried couple traveling together," when Keith and I went to New York City to see Broadway shows for spring break, but otherwise, it's been smooth.

"They've also never had sushi," I say to Keith, tossing my newly dyed dark red hair. Even though I just tried sushi for the first time myself, I enjoy flaunting how adventurous I am.

"Ew, shooshi," Mom pronounces it. "No, thanks." Her face scrunches up in disgust, then springs to delight as she takes a bite of her chicken parmesan. Her lipstick fades with each chew, and her sparkly white sweater blinds me every time it catches the light. Her eyes bug as she remembers something.

"Oh! The other day, we got a letter from the HOA!"

My parents moved from their Raleigh apartment to a house in a rural chic community near Chapel Hill the summer before my sophomore year in their quest to follow me wherever I go.

"The letter asked us to remove the fake flowers from our front yard. Well, I had no idea that was a no-no, so I rushed right out and took them down," she says, mortified.

"That's weird, Mom. Who cares about fake flowers?" I say, chewing on my prime rib.

"Are you still hosting a Bible study out there, Dawn?" Keith asks.

I've realized that the brand of Christianity Keith grew up with is more watered down than mine. It's more like a gentle hug of knowing the meaning of it all, rather than my family's rigid, paranoid version.

"I am," she replies. "This couple from New Jersey, the Russos, come every week. They moved here to be closer to their son, who works in the Triangle. They are baby Christians, so I have so much to catch them up on, but they're learning." She rolls her eyes with the exhaustion of knowing more than most people.

"That's great, Mom." With her encyclopedia-like knowledge of the Bible, she must be a great teacher.

"Are you still going to that End Times Bible study?" she asks me.

"No, not anymore. I got too busy with school," I say, keeping my eyes down, hoping my true thoughts aren't showing.

I attended a weekly study of Revelation for a while led by a guy from my parents' church. We would meet at his office at 7:30 am, and by 9 am, the whiteboard in his company's conference room would be covered in verses, names, drawings, and lines connecting everything, the kind of delusional man's collage of photos, maps, pins, and strings in a movie.

"And how are your engineering classes going, Keith?" Dad asks, seizing a rare pause.

"Well, Sir," he drawls, "each semester gets harder and harder, but ah think ah'll manage." Keith initially earned a bachelor's degree in technical theatre and worked in the field for a few years until he realized that theatre life couldn't afford him the house and family that he wanted someday. He's gone back to school to be an engineer. Even though I don't care about having a house or a family, his maturity is such a turn on.

"And how's school going for you, Susan?" Mom asks.

"I lucked out again this semester with all Tuesday/Thursday classes!"

And by lucked out, I mean I logged on the second you can sign up for classes, so I could curate my dream schedule, as any self-respecting control freak would.

"I'm loving my philosophy of religion class, but I'm the only one defending Christianity in it now. It started with this one guy and me giving the Christian answers to the big questions, but now it's just me. Last week, at the end of class, he threw up his hands and was like, 'I give up! I guess I would believe whatever I was raised in, and since I grew up Christian, that's what makes sense to me.'"

"I'm surprised you like this class," Mom says, her brow furrowed. "Seems like a waste of time."

"Well, it's challenging in a good way, like how do you logically arrive at what you believe? I-"

"But that's not what it's about, Susan," she jumps in. "It's about faith, and the irrefutable truth of the Bible."

"But if something is the truth, it should be obvious in every way, right? Biblically and logically," I press.

I can feel her getting frustrated, and the men withdrawing.

"I'm really proud of my first paper. We had to argue against John Godfrey Saxe's poem about these blind men touching an elephant. They're arguing over what an elephant is because each man is touching a different part: the tail, a tusk, the trunk. It's a metaphor for religion because-"

"Oh, the old 'all religions are the same' thing," Mom says, rolling her eyes.

"Well, like what if Muslims are calling 'Allah' in their language, what we call 'God', and Jews call 'Yahweh'? What if we're just using different words for the same thing?"

I'm risking triggering her "Muslims are evil" speech (she was outraged when colleges put the Quran on their summer reading list), but I would be so much happier if I didn't have to believe that so many people are wrong or bad.

"They're not the same, Susan," Mom says definitively with gritted teeth and piercing eyes.

"How did you argue against it in your paper?" Dad asks, speaking up over the din of a busy restaurant.

"I argued that there has to be some litmus test for truth. Saxe's poem makes an interesting point, but by his logic, anyone can make up anything, and we can just call it another part of the elephant, whether it is or not. An elephant is still a specific, finite thing."

"Hm," Dad says into his plate.

"You missed your calling, Susan, not being a lawyer," Mom says coolly.

"Y'all going to see Susan in *Pippin* next weekend?" Keith asks, giving me a wink and rubbing my leg. "Ah'll be there opening night," he smiles.

I exhale, relieved our debate didn't escalate. My parents exchange a look.

"We'll see," Mom says. After seeing me say the F-word in one college show and passionately kiss in the next, my parents have stopped attending my performances.

"So, we have this new girl, Kimmy, at Dance Design," the retail shop I work at, "and she is from the deeeeeep south."

"Oh, here we go, what'd she do?" Keith says, good-naturedly.

"It's how she talks. She says pillow with an 'e': pellow! 'Ah laid mah head down on mah pellow!'"

"What?" Mom laughs. Dad starts to smile.

"And 'UM-brella,' emphasis on the 'UM.' 'It's rainin', so ah need mah UM-brella!'" I'm killing with my over-the-top Southern accent. "How do you say it, Keith?" I say, poking him.

He grins sheepishly.

"UM-brella."

We all laugh as our slices of cheesecake arrive, mine with "Happy birthday!" written in chocolate syrup on the plate.

After saying goodbye to my parents and getting in Keith's

car, he asks, "It's your 21ˢᵗ birthday, sure you don't wanna go somewhere and get a drink? Say ya did? Mah 21ˢᵗ was somethin' else," he laughs.

"Nah, I'm fine. I'm going to the early service at church tomorrow, because we have tech for *Pippin* at noon."

I don't attend my parents' evangelical megachurch in Raleigh anymore but have settled on a small, non-denominational one nearby, an ever-so-slight rebellion. I still have to calculate tomorrow's tithe, the Biblical command to give 10% of your income to the church.

"God can do more with your 10% than you can do with the 100%!" our old pastor used to say.

I'll never forget when I was 12 or so, my parents clarified that it was 10% of new income, not 10% of everything every single week. I was gobsmacked at how much I'd been over-tithing on my allowance.

Keith drops me off at the shabby two-bedroom apartment that I share with another student who has a cat, an aquarium, two chinchillas, and her walls decorated with swords and old dungeon-looking keys. The swords came in handy one night when I was home alone, and someone banged on our door at 2 am and jiggled the handle for a while. I ran to her room, yanked a sword off the wall, and stood facing the door with my cell phone in one hand and a sword in the other until they went away.

"All righty then. Well, ah'll be there opening night," Keith grins. "Break a leg."

"Thanks, see you then!" I smile and brace myself for the cold, our first North Carolina winter with snow. We lightly kiss goodbye.

Even though he's had sex with previous girlfriends, he respects that I am following God's order to wait until marriage. That decision was further solidified when some of the girls in my college's Christian group tearfully opened up one night about their shame and regret over losing their virginity. Some had lost it to boyfriends, but others' stories of losing their virginity seemed more traumatic. The whole thing seems so dangerous.

I unlock my apartment door, the worn knob loose in its socket, and hear a flurry of movement and gasping on the couch as my roommate and her boyfriend dive under a big blanket.

"Heeeeey, Laura," I giggle. "You're good, just passing by!" I hold my purse up to block my view of their probably naked bodies while I scurry across the living room past the cat, fish, and chinchillas.

"Happy birthday, Susan!" Laura laughs from under the blanket. I can hear Rob snickering.

Well, not everyone's waiting.

CHAPTER 13
U. OF F.E., PART 3

"I ALWAYS THOUGHT a girl's best friend was her mother!"
-*Marnie*

~22~

One month before graduating from college, Mom said I had to drive us to New York to visit Grandma Irene at her nursing home for a final goodbye.

"This weekend, Mom? *This* weekend?" I said to her incredulously, picturing the to-do list in my planner where the writing gets smaller and smaller. I have final papers, projects, tests, a speech to write, an apartment to pack, auditions, last get-togethers with my theatre pals…

It's not that Irene is dying, any more than any 98-year-old is dying, but this is the last time she'll be a drive away since my parents have decided to move back to no accents, no seasons, Central Coast California, the day after I graduate. Since Mom won't fly, this is goodbye.

If I had a post-graduation plan, my parents might have tried to follow me there, too, but I'm waiting to hear about several callbacks for tours, regional theatre productions, and internships.

As we pull up to the industrial, gray nursing home, my brain is at capacity thinking about each of those potential trajectories, plus my to-do list, plus the big one: what to do about Keith?

Recently, we were walking hand-in-hand at the mall when he started to pull us toward a jewelry store, mumbling something about rings. Panic tore through my body at the prospect of settling down with him in the country house his father has planned for him, so I jerked us back to keep walking.

Not when I'm this close to being free!

His father's southern accent, which sounds like clipped, twangy barks, is so thick that I can't understand one word he says to me. I just say "School's going great, thanks" when he addresses me and hope I covered it.

With one foot in my vanishing college life and one foot lunging into my much-anticipated but unknown future, I don't have an extra foot for Grandma.

"Knock, knock, Irene," the nurse says as her knuckles tap the open door to Grandma's tiny room. Its white walls and few contents: a hospital bed with small tables on each side, a few chairs, and a walker, are painted urine yellow by the morning sun.

Seeing her thin, frail frame in the bed, coiffed, blue-white hair, streaks of blue eyeshadow, and coral lipstick, takes me back to a year ago when I helped her fly home to Elmira after visiting us, and she had a stroke on the plane. The airline staff thought I was being dramatic when I calmly but firmly told them she needed medical attention after recognizing the signs of stroke (thanks, Dad) when we landed.

Grandma's been at this nursing home ever since, and Mom has never forgiven herself for letting her fly since the elderly are apparently at risk for blood clots at 35,000 feet.

"Guess who's here to see you today! Do you know who this is?" the nurse asks my grandma, pointing to me.

I smile at her from the foot of her bed, my hair back to its natural dark blonde and in a pony, wearing a flowery teal and orange dress that my mom bought me, but is actually cute.

Irene looks me over, her blue eyes squinting behind her large, clear glasses, then she smiles pleasantly.

"Clementine. That's Clementine," she chirps confidently. Her large, bony hands with thick blue veins, adorned with large rings, fidget, as they always have, on her lap.

I nod and smile back rather than correct her, beginning the necessary mental separation from the scene.

I'm not here. This isn't happening.

Detach Mode activate: my body fades from the room, and my eyes turn into a camera, simply recording the events. Sure, my heart will do its whole feeling rigamarole at some point, but that could be days from now, maybe years if I'm lucky.

The nurse gives me a sorry-she-got-your-name-wrong look, then says, "Well, I'll let you all visit," before leaving the room.

I stay standing, silent. Mom, in a simple white shirt and gray sweater, sighs and sits next to Grandma's bedside, then pulls a gift out from her enormous lavender purse and starts to lose it.

"Mom," she says, her voice shaking, "I want to give you this Bible."

She starts to hand the new, leather-bound book to her and then stops as her face scrunches up and she starts sobbing with her head down. Grabbing a Kleenex from the bedside table, she dabs her eyes, careful not to mess up her makeup, and holds the tissue over her nose while she collects herself.

"Whenever you want some comfort," Mom says through tears, "read this."

I glance at the other bedside table, where a worn, red Bible already rests next to a framed photo of my senior high school picture. Grandma has been a born-again Christian since Mom became one and talked her into it, but I suppose it's nice to give a tangible, meaningful final gift.

What do nonreligious people do in times like these? Death and the afterlife are easier pills to swallow with the assurance of heaven.

"Oh, okay," Irene says amiably, but I'm not sure she knows what's going on.

Mom starts to hand her the Bible, then, realizing Grandma probably can't lift it, rests it on the bedside table.

They've had a tumultuous relationship, and each one would talk my ear off about the other.

"Grandma needs to learn to cast her cares on the Lord. She's still bitter over burying two husbands," Mom would say.

"Your mother never used to be this heavy. I mean, each bun is like this!" Irene would say to me with her hands indicating how wide each of my mom's butt cheeks was.

To me, though, she was the perfect grandma: kind, doting, full of presents even though she had little money, and so much warmer and easier to talk to than my severely reserved grandparents on my dad's side.

"There's a bookmark in there for you, too," Mom says, then clears her throat to get her voice strong. "It's got Psalm 23 on it. Whenever you need it, that can be your prayer: 'The Lord is my Shepherd; I shall not want-'"

She breaks down again, and I hate that we cry the same way: every feature on our face expands until we look like a clown. The difference between us is that I never let anyone see me cry, unless it's on stage, the only safe place for emotions.

Grandma just watches Mom blankly, her hands fidgeting. Mom eventually pulls herself together, grabs her purse, and then looks at me.

"Let's get going." It's a full day's drive back to North Carolina. "Goodbye, Mom," she says tightly as she stands up.

"Bye, Grandma," I mumble, as my body fades back into the room.

"Bye now. See you again soon," she replies with a vacant smile, waving.

On my last glimpse of her, the sadness of who she used to be and who she is now, and the fact that we're just leaving her here like this, starts to rise from my gut, but before it reaches my throat or God forbid my eyes, I push it back down.

"Mom, wanna do McDonald's for breakfast?" I say once we leave her room.

An Egg McMuffin and an iced vanilla latte, her favorites, will cheer her up, right?

They don't. On the drive back, Mom is unusually quiet, staring out the window like a tired old dog with a blonde bob. I try to lose myself in the freeway, but all that I was processing pre-visit comes roaring back to the forefront.

I've had a one-track mind for as long as I can remember: be an actor. Ironically, it's the one place I can be myself. Nothing can get in the way of that. I've never been the girl who daydreams about her wedding or being a wife and certainly not a mother, but I never perceived marriage as the end of my independence and dreams until it became a possibility with Keith. How to reconcile that with Christianity's tenet that I can't have sex until I'm married, I have no idea.

If I don't want to get married, but I can't have sex unless I'm married, I guess I'm never having sex?

Maybe my problem is that I'm actually a robot who can't feel things like grief over Grandma or love for Keith. I was certainly infatuated in our early months, and his presence offers a comforting stability. But I often feel like I'm playing a part: a good girlfriend would say this now, a good girlfriend would do that. Maybe marriage is so scary because I would have to drop the act at some point and actually be myself.

God, who wants that?

People in relationships say how great it is not being alone anymore, but I find being alone such a relief. No masking. No placating.

As we whiz past the Welcome to North Carolina sign on I-85, Mom is snoring in her fully reclined seat, and a memory of Keith pops into my head: the time he proudly showed me the guns his family, who have been in one county for generations, used in the

Civil War. Being a Californian with no previous connection to that side of our nation's gruesome history, I was utterly shocked.

Noticing my stunned face, he said sheepishly, "Mah family gave up their slaves before they were forced to."

That's it! I'll let him down gently with the location angle: "Keith, your life will always be in North Carolina, and mine will not."

Postscript

In the year she would have turned 100, we got the call that Grandma Irene died peacefully in her sleep. I instantly burst into tears and was filled with regret.

Why hadn't I called her more? Why hadn't I flown to visit her? How could I have let someone so kind and generous to me my whole life slip from my radar when it wasn't convenient or comfortable anymore?

Detach Mode always catches up with you.

CHAPTER 14
IT'S A FLAT, FLAT, FLAT, FLAT EARTH

"RETURN to the land of your fathers and to your kindred, and I will be with you."
  -Genesis 31:3

~22~

What's more depressing than going back to your hometown jobless after graduating from college? Going back to your hometown jobless after graduating from college, and moving in with your parents.

Last month, on a sunny Carolina day in May, I delivered an impassioned speech about our bright future (ha) at the Dramatic Art department's graduation ceremony at UNC-Chapel Hill, parted ways with my boyfriend so I could be free to pursue my career (Ha!), then helped my 65-year-old parents do the cross-country drive back to California and get settled into their/our (HA!) new home. With nothing else better to do yet, despite voracious morning online searches for auditions/gigs/anything halfway entertainment-related to escape this stuck and frustrating existence, I've just stayed. Today, it's another Taco Bell lunch with Mom, and she's buying.

"Have you heard from Kohl's yet?" she asks, breaking off a piece of her tostada. I applied there yesterday out of desperation.

I could have worked at Kohl's without going to college. What was the point?

"Nope," I murmur into my soft tacos.

Oh, God, what if Kohl's doesn't even want me?

"Well, hopefully you can work there until your tour," she says, all smiles.

I turned down some unpaid internships to accept the best gig I was offered: a West Coast tour of *Babes in Toyland*, the children's musical, for the holidays. I was thrilled to book a tour, albeit a short one, but the October start date feels like an eternity away.

"This morning, I responded to an ad on Craigslist for a kids' acting teacher in L.A. for some summer classes. Maybe I could do that before the tour," I say with a shrug.

Teaching kids sounds dreadful, but I'm looking for any excuse to test out actor life in the big city. L.A. seems like a sinkhole of fake, flakey, gorgeous airheads, but it's a lot warmer than New York. You can take the girl out of California….

"Well, I'm so happy to be back here, aren't you?" my mother sings, looking out the window, comforted by this familiar, balmy, achingly slow way of life. Her bubble of blonde hair bounces as she chews.

"Not really," I say, as Taco Bell Fire sauce drips down my chin. I've got a hat pulled low over my eyes so no one recognizes me.

"So, went to college far away, and now you're back, huh?" I dread my hometown friends saying.

Throughout my childhood, our town of peach stucco houses with Spanish tile roofs and chain restaurants surrounded by rolling green hills was prophesied to be a haven for the End Times. For me, it's just a haven for allergies.

"Ugh. What am I going to do here? There's nothing for me to do," I whine, looking out the Taco Bell window forlornly. I recently made it to the final five for Belle in a production of

Beauty and the Beast in L.A., and when I sang about her provincial life at the callback, I thought, "I feel ya, sister."

Mom purses her lips, sits back in the booth, and folds her arms. She's had enough.

"Well, at least you weren't junked around in high school like I was."

Here we go. The grievance I've heard a million times.

"When I was a freshman, and my father was diagnosed with lung cancer, the doctor said, 'Go where it's warm, it'll be easier on his body.' Well," she says with a huff, her eyes wide, "the culture shock! I had to leave all my friends in Elmira, where people are normal, and go to high school in Inglewood," she says with disgust. "The girls all looked like movie stars! They were doing their makeup in class, painting their nails, not paying any attention to the teacher at all! Their hair was beautiful. They dressed provocatively. It was just horrible!" She punches the end of each sentence with a head rattle.

"Then just when I start to make some friends, my parents miss Elmira so badly, back we go during my senior year. I'm way behind because of how dumbed down everything was in Inglewood, and my old friends don't even recognize me."

She shakes her head and looks away as her eyes get red. She's never recovered from the profound insecurity of those teen years.

"We never did that to you, now did we?" she says, looking back at me, arms still folded.

"No, Mom," I sigh, keeping my eyes down.

But I wish I had gone to high school in Inglewood for its proximity to professional auditions! And I attended high school alongside model-gorgeous girls, too, but it didn't give me a complex.

Maybe hers was just a different time for women. If you couldn't trap a man with your looks, what good were you? I can't relate to her attachment to friends either, but that could be my   I'm-dead-inside-and-can't-feel-anything-for-anyone problem.

I've always seen my life as a narrow path lying before me with only room for me. A close friend or boyfriend joins the path for a time, so I contort myself to make room, but eventually, they return to their path, and I'm relieved.

A group of teens takes over a big booth next to us, and their high-energy chatter eats up our silence as we finish eating.

Yes, that's who should be at Taco Bell on a Wednesday afternoon.

On the drive home, my phone rings.

"Who's that?" Mom says from behind the steering wheel.

"Uh, I don't know the number."

Please be a job. Please be a job.

"Hello?" I answer.

"Hi, is this Susan Huckle?" a woman's voice says.

"Yeah, that's me."

"Hi, Susan, this is Leticia with StarKids in L.A. You applied to be a teacher with us, yes?"

"Yes, I did," I say excitedly, feeling anxious hope start to rise. "Yes, I'm used to working with kids because I was a private tutor when I was in high school," I say truthfully when Letitia asks me about my experience with kids. "I love working with them!" I lie.

I listen closely as she explains the class times, locations, pay, start date, and required background check. By the time the call is over, we're home, and I'm perched on the edge of the couch. Mom stops washing dishes in the kitchen and walks into the living room. Dad is napping in his room, his comically loud snoring audible.

"Well? What happened?" she says, her yellow rubber gloves dripping with soapy water.

"Once I pass the background check, the job is mine! My first class will be next Thursday. I guess I'm moving to L.A.!" Anxious hope explodes into victorious excitement.

"Oh," she says. Her eyes flicker with disappointment and fear. "Well, good! Good for you!" she says, putting on a brave face for me.

I race to my laptop in my bedroom with a new mission: find a place to live in L.A.

Life.

Has.

Begun!

CHAPTER 15
LAST STOP BEFORE FALLING OFF THE FLAT EARTH: LA-LA LAND

"TIP the world over on its side and everything loose will land in Los Angeles."

    -Frank Lloyd Wright

~23~

My roommate Vanessa and I thoroughly embarrass ourselves at a dance audition way out of our league, then stumble into the theatre's lobby after being cut, barely able to contain giggles over how ridiculous we must have looked. As we get out of our character shoes and put sweatshirts and jeans on over our tights and leotards, she gives me that look: pleading eyes with a faint, growing smile.

"Yes," I say, knowingly.

Even though it's almost 10 pm, we hastily grab our bags brimming with sheet music, dance shoes, and headshots and race to her car to get to our happy place: the Pacific Coast Highway, miles and miles of ocean view road that make any day better.

After falling in love with the endlessly stimulating characters, businesses, and neighborhoods of L.A. last summer (when I wasn't begging too shy or too out-of-control kids to act), I moved right back after the tour, which was a two-month whirlwind of early shows for kids, sightseeing, long drives in the van, and the silliness and pettiness that only 20-somethings stuck with each other can get into. We really put the 'Babes' in *Babes in Toyland*.

Vanessa cranks the radio and opens all the windows as we zoom along the 10, beach-bound in her beat-up Jetta with a cracked bumper held on by duct tape and covered in stickers exclaiming "Save the Rainforest" and "Coexist" in various religious symbols.

We sing along with Van Halen's "Running with the Devil," unfazed by the chilly winter air giving us goosebumps. We've been trashing that dance call ever since we got in the car.

"Oh, you want a double after all those turns in different directions? Please!" I say, mouthing off to the choreographer who just cut us as if he's in the car with us.

"Yeah, go fuck yourself! And your doubles!" Vanessa hollers out the window. The air gets saltier as we approach the coast.

We end up at a Manhattan Beach bar with bottomless chips and salsa (free dinner!) and order beers. I tested the drinking waters on tour, enjoying a glass of white wine or a white Russian (sometimes two!) with the cast on our days off, and found that life feels lighter half a drink in.

An attractive young guy with dark hair and eyes flashes us a smile from across the bar. I instantly break eye contact with him while Vanessa flashes back a playful smile and sultry eyes.

"You're still seeing Charlie, right?" I ask, keeping my eyes down.

"Fuck no. I found out he's still sleeping with his ex. I can't believe it, after how great the sex was. I've never seen anyone come so hard when their asshole's licked."

Look normal, look normal, look normal, I tell my face when she says things like this.

"He's cute," she whispers to me, releasing her long, brunette hair from a ponytail. She tosses a big chunk to one side.

"Mm," I manage, avoiding the bar guy's eyes at all costs. Every week, there's a new cute guy with her, but I've never felt that instant attraction.

Sure, a guy may be cute, but is he an idiot? Is he funny? Is he a horrible person? Doesn't that matter more than cute?

Vanessa and I pull out our planners and talk shop, comparing notes rapid fire on audition postings, agents taking submissions, classes friends recommended, and random gigs. Searching for acting work is a nonstop pursuit in a million directions. When we exhaust all that, she broaches her second favorite topic.

"So, what's the latest with your parents?" she says, putting her planner away.

I'm finding that when I open up about them, friends look at me perplexed.

I know they can be extreme, but is it worse than I realize?

I mistakenly assumed everyone grew up with some religious framework and an older generation's morality. When people tell me they drink with their parents, my mind is completely blown.

"Oh, you'll love this. My mom is now keeping a log of activity at their next-door neighbors' house because she thinks they're drug dealers. If that isn't textbook busybody, I don't know what is." I wash down a salsa-drenched chip with my beer.

"Why does she think they're drug dealers?" She laughs and takes a swig.

"Well, all these different people in expensive, fancy cars stop by for short visits, apparently."

Never mind that Mom's hated their blaring mariachi music ever since they moved in.

"What's the point of the log, though?" she says, while flashing another smile at the bar guy.

"Well, she's writing down license plates, times of visits, and descriptions of people, and I guess she thinks it'll be helpful to the police or something."

I tried to offer other explanations for these visits: "Maybe they have a big family? Or lots of friends, Mom?" But once she's convinced, that's it. I shake my head, then catch the server's eye and indicate we'd like more chips, please.

Starving actors over here.

"Wow," Vanessa says, dumbfounded. "My mom just takes pills to get through the day. She thinks we don't know about it, but we do." She grabs a lipstick and compact out of her purse.

"Really?"

Are all moms on pills?

"Yeah, she wants everyone to think she's the perfect Christian wife and mother. What a bunch of bullshit," she says. Vanessa's a Buddhist these days. She finishes applying Vixen Red to her lips. "I'll be right back."

"Get it, girl," I whisper as she saunters over to the bar guy who has a beer waiting for her.

I chomp some chips while I ponder. I'm afraid that looking too closely at my parents' character flaws will infect the religion they instilled in me. I'm in too deep. I have to stick with what I know and play it safe.

But where are those End Times already? And my dad's healing? Why are some of my non-Christian friends just as loving, if not more than, the best Christians I know? If I weren't a Christian, what would I believe? Why can't I flirt with a cute stranger? Does anyone else think about everything all the time like I do?

I gulp my beer. Vanessa returns victorious.

"We're meeting up in Hollywood Saturday night!" she says, sitting down next to me.

"Fun!" Every fling of hers ends in disaster, but I always hope the next one will be different.

She adds the date to her planner. "Hey, let's go see Cary's improv show tomorrow after work. He's funny, it should be good."

"Sure," I say, too quickly. I had a dream last night about looking deep into Cary's eyes with our foreheads touching. We met him at our new job, a call center where we ask for donations to organizations that would outrage my conservative mother if she knew, like NARAL Pro-Choice America and Dems for Hillary. It's flexible, a must for an actor's day job, and I've justified it this way: they're going to pay someone to do this whether it's me or not. Luckily for my mother and not so much for the organizations, I'm terrible at it.

Cary and I always sit together and laugh nonstop between calls. It's no wonder he's in so many commercials with his loveable schlub type and gift for improv. We bonded over growing up in large Pentecostal churches, but I get the impression he's not a Christian anymore.

Vanessa and I take the long way up the coast back to our apartment in the valley, alternating between singing, laughing, and plotting. Just before we turn inland, I pause to take in the mysterious beauty of the moon's reflection on the dark lapping water. Despite all the ways that this city challenges who I was raised to be, it feels like home.

CHAPTER 16
COLLISION COURSE
WITH THE FLAT EARTH

"THE GREATEST SOURCES of our suffering are the lies we tell ourselves."

-Elvin Semrad

~23~

It's the middle of the night, and I am wide, wide awake. If my skull was hooked up to a brain scan, all four lobes would be on fire.

Has everything changed? Has nothing changed?

I'm sitting on the small, blue couch in Cary's brother's sparsely decorated living room, my cotton shorts and tank top drenched in sweat, yet I'm shivering under the heavy white blanket wrapped around me. I retreated here so I could hear myself think over Cary's roaring snores in the guest room. I look out the window of the adobe-style house for answers in the withholding navy sky.

Well, no lightning bolts yet.

Earlier today, I took a plane. Then a bus. Then a taxi. To tell Cary that I loved him back. As each mode of transportation brought me closer to him, to *it*, I grew surer of my decision. The night before he left for a two-week trip to visit his brother in Santa Fe, he confessed he loved me, with our foreheads touching just like in my dream. But I went mute. He excused himself to the bathroom when tears welled up in his eyes after I didn't say it back.

We've been friends for six months, dating for two, and he's the only person I've ever met who I can't get enough of. I love his curveball sense of humor, his relaxed presence, his stocky build, and his success as an actor. But the words "I love you, too" were caught in my throat because I was caught: caught between the relationship I wanted with him (*jump my bones already, you atheist!*) and the relationship I should want (two unmarried Christians, zero sex). If I said the words, I'd be admitting that I wanted to be all in. When I saw how hurt he was by my silence and felt an unbearable disconnection between us, I knew it was time to make the decision I'd been avoiding. And a phone call wouldn't cut it.

"Surprise!" I said with a tentative smile after exiting the taxi this afternoon and locking eyes with Cary, seated on the patio of his brother's restaurant.

Please look happy to see me, please look happy to see me.

The big smile on his face said it all, as did the fact that he eagerly introduced me to his brother, Patrick, who insisted I stay with them at his house. It was right out of a romantic comedy, if only the whole restaurant had cheered when we kissed and I whispered, "I love you, too," in his ear.

Now, I feel the same but different, older and younger, wrong but right, slightly sick to my stomach, and partly proud of myself. What just happened didn't blow my mind, like people say it does, but it wasn't painful, unlike my first gynecologist visit that I left bleeding and crying. At least some co-workers recently taught me how to use a tampon. I used to have to make up excuses for why I couldn't go swimming when I was on my period.

At 23, I've just lost my virginity.

That's like 50 in L.A. years.

As my mind races, a foreign feeling lingers in my body: the carnal nature I was taught to resist. It's animalistic, selfish, ravenous. How does that fit into my controlled, rational modus operandi? It was jarring to see that side of Cary, too. I switched into a new gear (Propagate the Species Mode?) and detached quickly, avoiding seeing or feeling too much, to protect the terrified child inside.

Keith would kill me if he found out how fast I gave it up for the next guy.

One year in L.A. unraveled 22 years of religious conditioning. Or maybe being a good Christian virgin was just my excuse to never be this vulnerable.

I pull my knees into my chest and wrap the blanket tighter around me, as I recall all the embarrassing prep that went into this rite of passage: shaving a new area, buying sexy underwear, and making sure to take my birth control pill at the exact time each day to ensure effectiveness for its primary purpose. I've been on it for years for mild acne.

Will I be cast aside now, just another notch in a belt, as I've been warned by every youth pastor?

A booming snore of Cary's hits my ears.

Well, he hasn't bolted yet.

All of a sudden, terror grips my vital organs. My heart skips a beat at the very thought of my parents finding out about this.

They would kill me!

Or I would die from disappointing them first.

Susan! Why are you thinking about your parents at a time like this? You should be afterglowing or something

But this is the unforgivable. No going back. No more pretending we're on the same side.

I search for the shame and regret I'm supposed to feel after committing this sin...but there isn't any. What I feel is... normal...for once. The shame I had about my ignorance and fear around sex is actually…gone! I've been on the boring side of the sex fence, peeking over at my peers, for years now.

I let out the biggest exhale of my life. My shoulders practically hit the floor. Then I close my eyes and bow my head.

Dear God, I know I have sinned. And it's a biggie. Please forgive me. I don't think you really care about swear words or drinking, as long as no one's getting hurt, but this one's a doozy. There goes my purity once and for all. The thing is, God, that I'm going to keep sinning, because I have found someone whom I want to have a real, intimate relationship with. Don't you want me to have that? I know, I know, you'd want me to be married first. But that's laughable in L.A., and the thought of getting married still gives me the willies.

How about this? We'll make a deal. As long as Cary and I stay together and he's the only one I ever have sex with, it'll be like we're married, right? A commitment of the heart instead of a piece of paper. That works for me. Does that work for you?

I open my eyes and look back at the navy sky through the window, hoping to see an old man's face appear in the stars and nod at me with approval and understanding. I stare for a few minutes. Nothing.

So, IF I'm actually okay with committing this sin, gulp, what about the whole paradigm?

Now Cary's deafening snoring sounds appealing.

Drown it all out, please.

I tiptoe back to the guest room and curl up next to him while my body and brain keep processing this defining moment in my life.

CHAPTER 17
THE FRAGILE
FLAT EARTH

"WHAT CANNOT BE SPOKEN to the (m)other cannot be spoken to the self."
- John Bowlby

~23~

The two-and-a-half-hour drive from L.A. to visit my parents blurs by as my mind gnaws on one sickening thought.

Will they be able to tell I'm not a virgin anymore? Is there a sign, an identifier you see once you're in the club, a shift that can be sensed?

I took the hottest, scrubbiest shower of my life this morning. If only I could don a sack.

No sexual being here!

Instead, I'm wearing a look that hopefully reads Super Duper Christian Virgin: simple gray shirt (not too tight!), a lavender skirt (not too short!), and plain hair and makeup (not too much!).

Nothing to see here, folks!

I park in front of their quintessential California ranch-style house, eggshell stucco with terracotta tile roof, and glance at the alleged drug dealers' house next door. It looks identical to my parents'.

Are they hiding things like I am?

A burning sensation *down there* grabs my attention, and I squirm to stop it. It's been intermittent since last night, but I'm hoping it just goes away. I turn off my birth control alarm and take the pill a tad early to avoid taking it in front of them and having to explain. I inhale deeply.

Just act like you're the Susan they want. Play the part. You can do that.

I knock our knock (da da da da da - da da) and the second Mom opens the door, I nervously launch into bemoaning the traffic until we take our seats on the two small couches that face each other in the living room. Every lamp is on, and all is white: ceiling, curtains, furniture, carpet, except Mom's salmon lipstick and all denim ensemble.

She seems normal. Nothing detected yet. So far so good.

"So, how's everything in L.A.?" she asks, when I finally run out of steam.

Well, I'm having sex now with the boyfriend I haven't told you about, so all the religious beliefs I've clung to my whole life are starting to unravel-

"Good news! I have a commercial agent now! I went to an open call, and they offered to represent me. So, I'm getting new headshots with someone they recommended next month," I say with a big 'ol smile.

"Oh, good! That's great!" she squeals.

She's always my biggest cheerleader. How could I ever let her down?

Dad nods with approval from his seat at the dining room table just past us, then returns to fiddling with his beloved lazy Susan (was I named after her?) of pills, some prescribed but mostly supplements he swears by. He prefers a removed perch from the conversation, where there's less pressure to talk.

"Vanessa and I closed that Edgar Allen Poe show we were doing in North Hollywood. It was pretty avant-garde with lots of movement and crazy makeup, but it was lots of fun," I say.

Actually, the volatile director was a nightmare, and we suspected he abused his wife, who was in the show with us.

"Good! And how's Vanessa doing?" she asks.

Well, she had a threesome with a married couple, and now they're getting divorced because of it. It's all very dramatic-

"She's well. We're putting together a fundraiser show for a short film she wants to make."

"And your new place is working out?"

It's a lot better than the sober living dorm-style halfway house I was at with Vanessa while we looked for an apartment. People were regularly carted out on stretchers for overdoses, and our roommate Carly paid the manager in blow jobs.

"Yup."

Now, what's a safe topic I can be honest about?

"I'm thinking about taking a yoga class. I know, that'd be so L.A.," I say in my best valley girl, "but Vanessa keeps raving about how great it is for flexibility and-"

Mom's smile drops.

"You know that's Satanic, right?" she chirps. "The jargon and words they use are conjuring the Devil."

Um, what?

"I think yoga is from India, so the words are just in the language there, Mom," I say slowly, carefully.

"No. It's straight from the pit of Hell."

I look over at Dad for some help here.

Surely, you don't think this, too?

Our blue eyes meet for a second, then he clears his throat and looks back down at that fascinating collection of pills. He's the only one she'll listen to, but he picks his battles.

Well, add yoga to the no-no list.

"How's everything at your church?" she asks, referring to the small, non-denominational Christian church in Burbank I started attending when I moved to L.A.

Well, I haven't been in a while because my new job performing at a theme park requires weekend availability, but last time we talked about this, you scolded me, saying church should be my priority.

"Good. Everyone's really nice there," I say. "Pastor Todd just talked about Christ's love for the church," I add, vaguely remembering the last sermon I heard.

"Ah, Ephesians 5:25," Dad contributes, as if he's playing a game show called "Name! That! Verse!"

"Yeah," I say confidently.

Sure.

"How's everything here, Mom?" I ask, eager to get the attention off of me.

"Well, next door is still the same old thing, lots of suspicious activity," she says, her eyes rolling in their direction.

"Tell her what happened last week," Dad says, amused, patting a notebook on the dining room table.

That must be The Log. Maybe he married her for the entertainment value?

"Oh! Right! This little woman in a fuchsia dress got out of this huge white BMW," Mom says, animating every detail. "Now we've never seen her before, mind you. She left in eight minutes! I clocked it! If that's not a drug deal, I don't know what is!"

Mom's got way too much time on her hands.

"Really?" I say, trying to look interested.

"All in broad daylight! It was about noon, right, John?" she says, looking back at him.

"Around there," he says. Just when he opens the notebook to check, with his thick, black-rimmed glasses hanging on the edge of his nose, the doorbell rings.

"Oh, that must be Dan and Betty! They said they'd stop by today when I told them you'd be here," Mom says, thrilled.

"Oh, great!" I say, getting up. This couple always brings out a wistful, light-hearted side of my parents when they talk about "the old days in Santa Barbara." They met in the '70s when Dan rented a room in my dad's beach house after being kicked out by

Betty. When she filed for divorce, my dad became Dan's divorce lawyer, too, until she dropped the case and they reconciled. I relish these rare glimpses into younger, shinier John and Dawn, before his stroke, before the End Times, before, well, me.

"I got some snacks for us, maybe you can help me with those later," Mom adds.

"Sure!" I bounce across the pristine white carpet, fling open the light wood door with a large glass oval in the center, and reveal a pair of middle-aged churchy people: he in a white button-down shirt and tan slacks with sun spots all over his bald head, she in a navy pantsuit with perky Laura Petrie hair.

"Susan!" Dan says, opening his arms. He towers down like a giraffe to hug me since he's 6'6" and I'm 5'2".

"Good to see you, sweetie!" says Betty. "Are you famous yet?" We laugh and embrace.

Betty grills me about my acting career as usual, and I love her for it. We are meandering to the couches when shooting crotch pain interrupts my train of thought, and I suddenly have to go to the bathroom and excuse myself.

It's a relief to drop the mask when I'm alone, but it's not a relief when I relieve myself. Just a small amount of pee slices its way out.

I probably just need to drink more water.

When I return to the living room, guzzling water, Dan says proudly, with a twinkle in his eye, "You know, your dad is a Christian because of me."

"I know," I say, smiling, looking back at Dad. This is Dan's favorite story to tell me. I cross my legs to contain the pain.

"Boy, he did not want to hear anything I had to say about Christ. 'Stop it! Enough!' he yelled one night. You know how your dad never raises his voice," he chuckles. "But I wore him down, and he finally came with me to church one Sunday."

Dad nods as his eyes moisten. "Everyone was so happy there. I'd never seen anything like it."

"That's when you prayed for the first time, right?" Dan says.

"I just said, 'God, if you're real, prove it.' I mean, I didn't know how to pray yet," he says, embarrassed by his naiveté at the time.

I can picture my dad's furrowed brow as he tries to intellectualize his first church experience, the way I have to analyze everything, too.

"I woke up the next day..." He looks awe-struck and overwhelmed. "Well, I know now that the burden of sin had been lifted, and that's why I felt this indescribable joy."

I've spent my whole life praying and feeling nothing. What's wrong with me?

"Then you met Dawn, and the rest is history. So, you're welcome," Dan says with a sly grin. They all laugh, but Dan laughs the hardest. Conversation continues with Christianity-related topics like church, Joel Osteen, and *The Purpose Driven Life*, and I sit back.

Snoozefest.

"I'll go get some snacks and drinks if anyone wants anything," I volunteer, escaping to the kitchen. Thrilled to have something to busy myself with, I'm creatively arranging crackers, apple slices, and cheese on a platter when the sound of Mom wailing pierces my ears. I freeze, facing the white tile backsplash, and audibly tune into the eruption of emotion behind me.

"You haven't been through what we've been through!" Mom cries in a high, quivering voice. "We've had to hold onto the Word of God and cling to Jesus through all this! You just wouldn't understand!" She blows her nose and sobs hard.

Whoa, how did we get here?

"Oh, Dawn, I didn't mean to upset you," Dan says gently. "I'm just sharing my theological perspective. God is always in control, so we're not going to change his mind." He chuckles at how obvious that statement is to him, then stops when no one else laughs. "I just hate to see you spend so much energy on getting John healed and beating yourself up since it hasn't happened yet."

Ah, ha. My parents must have been sharing how they still pray for and believe that Dad's paralysis will be healed.

"It has happened. In the spirit realm," Dad says softly, barely audible over the sound of Mom weeping. "I believe that I'm already healed."

My feet are still glued to the floor, so I can't see Dad's face behind me, but I can picture him saying that familiar phrase: uncharacteristic determination in his eyes, jaw and temples tight, speaking between shallow breaths.

While it's inspiring to witness my parents hope for the improbable, when I add up all the prayer meetings, the healers, the books, Dad's countless binders of printed out healing verses to meditate on, the millions of times he's muttered to himself, "I am healed. I am healed. I am healed in Jesus' name," as he walks around the house with his cane, dragging his limp left foot while his gnarled left arm and balled up fist awkwardly swing, I become profoundly sad. Whenever I have to cry as an actor, this is what I think about.

They go around in circles: Dan apologizes, Mom sobs, Dad tries to soothe her, repeat. If this were a play, it's time for a character to enter and relieve the tension with a one-liner.

It's my cue, but what's my line?

The apple slices are browning, so I pivot and gingerly approach the living room with a brave face and a full tray.

"Did anyone pray for snacks?" I quip. Dan and Betty give me lukewarm smiles while Mom bolts for the bathroom, probably to fix her running mascara, sniffling all the way. I set my work of art down on the glass coffee table, creating a startling sound that oddly amplifies the crotch pain I'd forgotten about. No one moves. All that's not being spoken is communicated via the eyes:

Dan and Betty: "Sorry we upset her."

Dad and I: "Sorry she's so easily upset."

This is why I lie by omission. No amount of honesty, about my life or when I disagree, is worth shattering her the way Dan just did. She can't even handle being surprised by a book. She always reads the last chapter first.

Maybe that's why she's obsessed with Revelation.

When Mom returns, the wayward mascara has turned into gray smudges under her eyes, and her energy is muted. So, Dan and Betty, my parents' last remaining friends, get up to leave. Mom treats friends like a diet, something you start with gusto and drop when it challenges you, and I fear Dan and Betty are the next Atkins.

I walk them to the door while Mom stays slumped on the couch and Dad just nods from his chair.

"Always great to see you, Susan," Betty says, hugging me at the door. Her eyes say, "Sorry Dan ruined everything."

"You, too!" I say, trying to be upbeat.

Oh, my God, pain, pain, pain, pain, I have to go to the bathroom right now.

I holler, "Thanks for stopping by!" and quickly shut the door. "I'll just use the bathroom and then probably get going, too," I chatter as I beeline for the toilet. "Beat the traffic and all, ya know."

Get me back to L.A., where people are normal.

During another excruciating tinkle, I overhear my parents dismissing Dan as simply being uninformed in this area of theology. As Mom recites the healing verses so dear to her, her energy returns. But now I've got to do something about this inexplicable five-alarm fire down below. As I dry my hands, Jesus' eyes in a frame above the towels catch mine.

God, are you punishing me?

...if you're even there?

I approach the living room, walking funny from the pain. Mom is now lying back in her white recliner in the corner and consoling herself with a favorite: *Battlefield of the Mind*, a charismatic movement book by a charismatic woman about how to make your thoughts more charismatic. Dad must have gone to his room to decompress. I notice on the kitchen counter an open bottle of what we usually only enjoy on Thanksgiving and Christmas: sparkling apple cider.

Mom's drowning her sorrows.

"Mom, I'm having this pain..." I'm almost too embarrassed to say it. "...when I pee."

She sets her glass down on a side table and looks up from her book, her eyes heavy and her face lackluster.

"It's probably a UTI," she says casually. "Grandma used to get them all the time. Cranberry juice helps. If it's that bad, you should see a doctor and get some antibiotics."

The pain is that bad, so I leave without ceremony, try my luck at the emergency room in town (thank you, parents' health insurance), and miraculously get seen right away. After testing a urine sample, the doctor confirms what Mom suspected.

"UTIs are common for sexually active women," he says clinically. "Just remember to urinate after intercourse every time to prevent them."

Remember? This is the first I'm hearing about this! Thanks, no one, for the heads up!

Wait.

My heart stops.

Was this just a huge giveaway to Mom that I am SEXUALLY ACTIVE?

I hit the road to L.A. after dark, armed with antibiotics and cranberry juice, and replay my exchange with Mom about the UTI over and over, frantically dissecting her expressions and body language for hints of the jig being up.

As the dry rolling hills on the sides of the freeway flatten into a dense urban landscape, the traffic worsens, and I exhale and relax back into the real me.

Nope, I've decided she didn't seem alerted in the least. After all, my widowed grandma apparently got them all the time, and she wasn't—

Hold the Depends, was Grandma SEXUALLY ACTIVE, too?

I roll my eyes at how ridiculous I'm being, throw back some cranberry juice, and call Cary. Wherever my personal spiritual journey takes me, as long as I keep her convinced that I'm still her agreeable, obedient, good little Christian girl, everything will be fine.

And I will pee after sex. Every time.

CHAPTER 18
THE DOMINOS FALL FLAT ON THE EARTH, PART 1

"I USED to be Snow White, but I drifted."
  -Mae West

~23~

"You can do this," I say, looking into my friend's petrified brown eyes, my hands on her shoulders. "You're doing the right thing."

"Thank...you...I..." Her childlike voice breaks. Her whole body shakes.

I give her a fierce hug just before she's led into an interrogation room at the police station near where we work to report the incest she suffered for years. Then I join the rest of our co-workers, who have come to be supportive, a diverse group of women in workout attire, on a bench in the lobby. We put our arms around each other while the heaviness of the moment drags our energy and faces down.

It's slower and quieter than I expected a police station to be. A cop's shoes squeak by us every so often, and sparse Christmas decorations attempt to cheer this serious place.

In the long breaks between our theme park shows, I've

learned that a staggering number of my co-workers have been sexually assaulted. One's drunk father got in bed with her multiple nights when she was a teen. One's brother forced himself on her until she was old enough to fight back. Several have had drugged drinks and dates go horribly wrong. Leave a group of women alone together long enough, and I guess this is what comes out. Our friend reporting abuse today is the first to tell law enforcement.

"I've got to go. I'm meeting my boyfriend and his parents for dinner," one says after an hour, obviously conflicted about leaving before our friend has returned from making her statement.

"Don't worry, I'll stay until she comes out," I say, leaning back against the cold, gray wall.

A VHS tape we watched at my Christian junior high plays in my head: an attractive, well-dressed woman told the story of a woman who was raped, discovered she was pregnant, then, with God's help, persevered through that experience to keep and love her rapist's offspring.

"That baby," she said at the end with a dramatic pause, "was me."

Mic drop.

Standing ovation.

Pro-life for life, baby!

But now, a decade later, when I think of one of my precious friends being forced to do the same, and at the young ages when some abuse began, I can't imagine it.

Only a monster would force a woman or a girl to go through that. I can't be a monster.

Then there's my married friend who desperately wants a child but keeps suffering miscarriages that require the procedure.

The church narrative of rape and incest as rare and abortion as something only a loose woman seeks is tragically, hatefully, viciously wrong.

When our friend returns to the lobby over two hours later, only Jen and I remain. I give her another big hug, mostly because I don't know what else to do, and the weight of her body falls on me. She is pale, and the tears look long dried.

"So how did it go?" I ask, tentatively.

"They said there's probably not much they can do," she replies in a daze.

"What?" Jen fires, immediately heated.

"I guess this type of thing is hard to prove," she says. With the little energy she has left, she tries to describe what was just explained to her about proof and statute of limitations, misdemeanor vs. felony, step-brother by marriage vs. blood brother, and all sorts of horrifying distinctions for trauma.

"You told them that he lives with you, right?" Jen says, with fire in her eyes. "That you have to see him every day."

I'm envious of her ability to speak her mind so quickly.

"Yeah," our friend replies softly, her head down.

"Well, I'm proud of you for telling them," I say, at a loss.

How can they just do nothing?

———

From the back of his unframed mattress that rests directly on frayed tan carpet, I'm watching Cary, in a ragged white shirt and boxers, sit slumped at the other end. His light brown hair is unkept since we just woke up, but his eyes are glued to his tube TV that sits on a Duraflame box. He softly cries tears of joy as our new president takes the oath of office, while my insides are being pulled in opposite directions.

"This is...historic," Cary musters through quiet sniffles. Luckily, the swearing-in ceremony has his full attention, so he's unfazed by my silence.

I want to cry, too, at the earth-shattering progress it is for this country, its history horrifically enmeshed with slavery and racism, to elect a Black man to the highest office. But after an upbringing in an extreme right echo chamber, I can't unhear Mom's snarl on the words 'Democrat' and 'liberal.' My parents made it clear that Democrats are mushy, airheaded freeloaders who forget to vote, have no brains for money, and hate religion and religious people.

When I was in college, and Bush was re-elected, all the liberal students were weeping in huddles at the quad, bemoaning the end of freedom and democracy, and it was the first time the other political side was humanized to me. It's like when you get to advanced American history, discover we're not always the good guys, then question if we ever were. When I told Mom about their tears, she spat, "Oh, let the bleeding hearts cry. Who cares?"

Today, she's probably crying.

I tune back into the TV:

"So help you, God?"

"So help me, God."

"Congratulations, Mr. President."

Cheering and applause explode.

Cary blows his nose.

I'm so ashamed.

You voted against this historic progress. How do you feel about that, Susan?

Uh, not so great, Self.

Remember last November when you also voted for Prop 8, the state ban on gay marriage, and all your dear gay friends from the theatre were devastated when it passed?

Now I'm crying. I want to crawl into a hole and die. I betrayed my friends. And for what? To follow the church's "love the sinner, hate the sin" catchphrase? It's easy to love my gay castmates, but I can't decipher why I'm supposed to hate their sexuality, especially when I encounter a homosexual relationship that looks just as loving and lasting as the best one in the church.

Susan, can you imagine if your gay friends made YOUR sins illegal, you hypocrite?

Ugh, Self.

Keeping my shame and naked body covered with Cary's Star Wars comforter, I lean forward and grab one of his spare tissues on the edge of the bed, glad that my crying unsuspiciously blends in with his.

Cary looks back at me, his eyes red. "This is something, isn't it?"

"Yeah," I manage.

Maybe I'm doing myself, my friends, and the country a disservice by blindly trusting my parents' take on politics.

And religion.

CHAPTER 19

THE DOMINOS FALL FLAT ON THE EARTH, PART 2

"MAN IS free at the moment he wishes to be."
  -Voltaire

~24~

It's Easter, and I'm going to church, SEXUALLY ACTIVE sinner that I am, for the first time in months. Old habits die hard. I can hear Mom's disdain for Christians who only attend church on the big holidays. She called them "in-name-only" Christians.

Just go. Fight the cognitive dissonance. You're always glad you went.

When I moved to L.A., I Googled "non-denominational Christian churches near me" to avoid the Pentecostal hold-onto-your-hats-here-comes-the-Second-Coming churches of my youth. I found the benign-sounding Victory Church after skipping over the Catholic search results. Of Catholics, Mom would say, "They're too hung up on Mary."

As any in-name-only Christian will tell you, you make up for the missed Sundays by going overboard on your outfit, so I'm in heels (ugh), pearls (fake), and a tan dress with white polka dots (my audition dress for classic musicals).

I'm singing along with the contemporary but still plodding worship songs in this small white chapel in Burbank with dark brown pews and wheat-colored carpet. My hands are raised in a supposed effort to connect with the unresponsive deity in the sky. In many ways, I'm just giving another performance.

Pastor Todd, dressed in a brown suit, looks like Robin Williams in *The Birdcage* with the same horrible mustache but none of the funny. Our exchanges have the same loop. He asks where I work. I say the theme park. He complains about how noisy that place is when he's golfing nearby. As the song ends, he takes the stage.

Oh, no. Not this part. I HATE this part.

"Let's now take a few minutes to greet each other," he says, as he always does after the first few songs. "Try to say 'hi' to someone new," he adds with a wink.

I specifically sat where I have a wide radius of no one around me so I can avoid the dreaded, painful awkwardness of this part of the service.

Oh, no. Someone's coming toward me.

No. No. Noooooo!

A sandy-haired man in khakis and a polo greets me with classic Christian fake face: wide smile, bright eyes, eyebrows perpetually raised. It screams for all to hear: "God is good! Aren't we blessed! Can I get an 'Amen!'"

"Hi! I haven't seen you here before! I'm Steve. Welcome!" he says enthusiastically, crushing my hand when he shakes it.

"Hi, I'm Susan. I've been coming here for a while."

"Oh, ya have? Huh. Well, great!"

We stare at each other with polite smiles and nothing else to say until a woman with frizzy blonde hair cuts in.

"Steve! Good to see ya!" she says. They hug, and he moves his attention to her, thank God. Just when I'm about to sit down and look busy on my phone, another man approaches me. He's sporting the other Christian face: squinted, serious eyes, deep forehead lines from intense daily prayer.

"Sarah, right?" he says, his jet-black hair shining under the bright lights.

"Close. Susan," I say, shaking his hand.

What is his name, dangit?

"How are you?" I ask.

"All is well, praise the Lord," he says, pained. "How about yourself?"

"Things are good. Yeah," I say, then both our heads bob to fill the silence.

Just admit it, Susan. These are not your people, and they never have been. You're supposed to be deeply spiritually connected to them, but you're just not. Your church is the theatre, and your tribe are the people in it: the funny, the gay, the open-minded, the real.

But, Self, if you're so smart, why do I always feel better after going to church?

Because it's a familiar routine? Because you desperately want to do the right thing? Because it makes your parents happy?

The worship music resumes, and I look around at the homogenous sea of churchgoers standing with their arms raised. Most have their eyes closed, and some have tears streaming down their faces. They sing with varying musical abilities, "Open the Eyes of my Heart, Lord."

Now would be the time to make an unnoticed getaway. I grab my purse and hold it while I decide between staying, going, or telling myself I'm going to the bathroom near the exit, only to walk right out. Not even being honest with yourself is the worst.

My feet ache from the heels; the fake pearls itch my neck, but I notice the beauty of the architecture: long, elegant windows, a calming, symmetrical pattern of wood beams on the ceiling with white paneling in between. This place does make my self-absorbed day-to-day problems fade away as I remember all I have to be grateful for and think about the bigger picture.

Listen to your body, Susan. You're sitting away from everyone. You're an adroit conversationalist with people you want to get to know, but here, you're tight-lipped. You can find places and practices that give you the same peace without these people, without the cognitive disso-nance this doctrine induces, without The Show. Maybe it's the inten-tional break from your routine and shift of perspective that is what has been therapeutic all along.

As the congregation takes their seats for the sermon and the pastor saunters to the pulpit, it's my last chance to make an unnoticed getaway.

Without making a conscious decision, my feet start walking to the exit, and I feel the thrill of autonomy spread as I get closer and closer to the door.

Goodbye forever, church.

As soon as I leave the building, the blazing L.A. sun baptizes me on a new, unknown, but chosen path.

CHAPTER 20

THE DOMINOS FALL FLAT ON THE EARTH, PART 3

"THIS ABOVE ALL: to thine own self be true."
  -William Shakespeare

~24~

Today I'm lunching with a friend in town: Christa, my spunky former co-star in a Christian North Carolina dinner theatre show where we served BBQ chicken to the blue hairs, then sang "Amazing Grace" for two hours.

I'm pretty sure she's a too-afraid-to-admit-it lesbian parading as a straight Christian, but at least she's a funny too-afraid-to-admit-it lesbian parading as a straight Christian. She has a long layover at LAX, so we're lunching at a Panera Bread near the airport, and I'm keeping careful control of the conversation and not mentioning Cary to avoid The Question.

"Remember when that enormous black snake was in the living room?" I say, chewing my salad. I still have the pictures we took of it balled up in the corner halfway up the wall of the actors' house we lived in for the two-month run of the show.

"Yeah! We were doing a *Will and Grace* marathon, and I started screamin' and prayin': 'Jesus, help us! We got a snake!'"

she hollers up to the sky in her crackly voice, her thick, short red hair wild. Our comedy-loving selves adored that TV show while our Christian selves were conflicted about the gay characters.

"But I had to take care of it," I remind her, remembering how I got a broom and tried to poke it towards the door.

"Remember when it lunged at you?" She laughs, making her baggy yellow T-shirt jiggle. She's always dressed sporty, and she's still got her softball muscles: rock-hard calves and noticeable biceps.

"Yes! That's when I screamed. You were no help at all, Christa. You just stood on the couch and prayed!" I laugh.

"I was casting out the Devil with my words, Susan! With my words!" She's holding her fork to the sky with conviction.

The snake eventually slithered out the door, because I was poking it all the way.

Before she stops laughing and asks The Question, I continue with our other greatest hits: the time we, two white girls, tried a church near our theatre that turned out to be a Black church. Christa jumped right in with everyone shouting "Hallelujah!" throughout the service, while I wondered if we were welcome.

There was the time we set up a handmade sign that read "Free food! God bless!" outside a supermarket with groceries we'd bought with our tithe money to give away. One woman and her kids snatched everything off the table and ran. We hadn't set an item limit, so we just shrugged and packed up earlier than expected.

"Have you ever thought of moving here?" I say when I exhaust memory lane. "I really love it. I've been able to support myself just from acting work for over a year now. I'm still trying to get a theatrical agent, but I've done some theatre and booked a few commercials."

Wow, hearing it out loud, I guess my dreams really are coming true.

"Awesome sauce. Nah, I don't think L.A.'s for me." She looks out the window nervously. It'd be a big leap from her small hometown in Florida, her home base for regional theatre gigs. She resumes eating her salad, the diet of actresses.

"You dating anyone?" she asks.

There it is. The Question.

We used to have achingly vulnerable talks about what a godly woman can and shouldn't do physically with a boyfriend:

Kissing? Fine.

French kissing? Probably not.

Taking clothes off? Frowned upon.

Absolutely no touching inside bathing suit lines, a.k.a. The Bikini Rule.

Unwed Christians could run the gamut from not even holding hands to doing absolutely everything except vaginal penetration, but that was our consensus. Christa seemed content to do as little as possible.

"Uh, yeah, I, uh, I have a boyfriend," I stammer.

Of a year-and-a-half now.

"Oh! Congrats! You haven't lost your V card, right?" she says confidently, pointing her fork at me.

Time stops. With her fork suspended in the air, the busy restaurant paused, and my face frozen with tension, I flash back to when our beliefs were perfectly aligned a few years ago, then fast forward through my life since then, like a flip book showing my evolution via incremental pages, and I realize that I've grown lightyears away from the person I was.

Oh, Christa, my Virgin card is long gone. And I'm starting to resent all the shame, fear, and excess anxiety around sexuality that the church pummeled into us. Sex is a complicated rite of passage for most people, but it doesn't have to involve God damning you, too.

Also, if you're a lesbian, that's all gravy.

Time resumes. Panera customers mill about, background chatter picks back up, and Christa awaits an answer.

"No, no, of course not," I lie, looking down at my salad, hiding my eyes. My neck feels hot and starts to sweat. "How about you? Seeing anyone?"

"No, nothing yet," she says in her scrappy way. Her eyes also stay hidden in her salad.

When she asks more about Cary, I focus on the commercials he's done and emphasize his Christian upbringing, leaving out his evolution, too. By then, it's time to get her back to LAX for her flight, so we leave.

Instead of unpacking why I lied, I quickly spin our lunch in my mind as a funny story for Cary later.

Cary doesn't laugh at the "V card" part, despite my comedic delivery.

Buffalo sauce drips on his shirt as we nosh on a late-night dinner of wings and beer on the tiny patio of my shoebox-sized studio in NoHo. A few stars glimmer through the light pollution, and the sounds of traffic and drunks fade to the background. It's an ordinary night for an extraordinary epiphany.

"You don't still think it's wrong, do you?" he says seriously, and it's the first time I'm realizing that my religious/sexual/political/life confusion may be affecting someone other than me.

"No, I guess not," I say, letting *her* answer for once. *She* is either the new me or just the real me who's grown in courage and dominance, no longer too frightened to speak up. *She* has no problem at all with pre-marital sex and is frankly more concerned now about people who wait. I lied to Christa not out of shame over losing my V-card but to avoid conflict.

I should work on that someday.

"And the Bible stories, I mean, come on," he says, shaking his head, adding their absurdity to the discussion. "A talking snake? Jonah and the whale? Noah's ark?" He rolls his eyes.

Only since I've been in L.A. have those stories been uttered with disdain.

"I guess I don't know," I say, gnawing on a wing, uttering *her* uncertainty, no, *my* uncertainty, for the first time.

"Susan, no one knows. Everyone's just pretending they do." He takes a big bite of a wing. "Except for agnostics," he adds through a full mouth.

What if… Ouch.

What if I… It hurts.

What if I don't have to have all the answers? What if it's okay to not know?

A weight the size of a boulder that's been crushing my heart lifts, and the impossible mental computation of how to make my new experiences add up to Christianity comes to an abrupt halt. In the background of every single day since I lost my V card, that equation has been screaming at me to be solved: how to reconcile my now broader perspective with the narrow one I was taught.

Mom's dismissal of agnostics as "wishy washy idiots" rings in my head, but that doesn't stop the word from resonating for the first time deep in my live-and-let-live soul that hates feeling like I have to convert people or condemn them. When you call yourself a Christian, you're expressing absolute certainty, and if there's one thing I'm certain of, it's that I'm not sure.

When I was a child, rules and fantastical stories were easy to accept. As an adult in a complex, diverse, random world, those rules and stories seem downright laughable, and I'm ashamed I foolishly held onto them this long.

"To not knowing," I say, holding my beer up, with chicken stuck in my teeth.

"To not knowing," he repeats with a grin.

As our beer bottles clink, I block out the image of Mom's sneer that I imagine she would have if she were witnessing this: two sinners toasting to ignorance.

I, on the other hand, freeze frame in my head the moment I was free.

As the night wind picks up and sends us inside, an unsettled feeling lingers: the knowing that at some point I should stand for something more than not knowing. But for tonight, letting go of the lifelong label "Christian" is enough. Baby steps.

Later that night, I'm about to hit 'Send' on an email when my eyes stop and hold on the last line, my signature for years. Someone once advised I change it to be more professional, and I ignored their advice to stand by my principles.

Ha!

I stare at it for a while, then go to my email settings and scroll down to the signature text box. I delete the "God bless," part and leave just "Susan."

I hope my parents don't notice.

ACT II

Five Years Later

CHAPTER 21
FLAT TIMES AT EARTH HIGH

"IF YOU BELIEVE IN JESUS, you'll believe in anything."
 -Marc Maron

~29~

Fuck, this orgy scene gets me wet. Even at a Sunday matinee of this original musical based on *The Picture of Dorian Gray* on a blistering July day. The dim, blue lighting and sensual music make me forget how dusty and cold the floor is that we're all writhing on in this dingy 99-seat theatre in Hollywood.

My statuesque friend Toni, in her glistening dark blue gown, softly sings stage left as the Demon character:

"A soft touch,

A kind word"

My sweat-soaked, skimpy, gold costume sticks to my skin as I grope and lick my fellow ensemble members center stage. The direction given to us for this song, where Dorian descends into hedonism, was "Go for it," so we do.

"A quick glance,

"Another chaaaaaaance"

Just when I'm caressing someone's face and another's thigh, I remember I'm visiting my parents tomorrow. Buzzkill.

When are you going to stop being such a fucking pussy, Susan, and be honest with them?

That's when the sultry gaze of my gorgeous pal, playing Dorian, steals my attention. He looks like a suave, svelte duck, and I pull him down to the ground.

Ugh, why does he have to be gay?

We lock lips, and I don't let go, playing our game of chicken to see who'll break the kiss first. We go longer and longer each night, and this is why I'm an actor. Forget being an artist or a storyteller, shit like this is a blast. The last time I had this much fun on stage was when I played Janet in *The Rocky Horror Show* a few years ago. Orgy scenes are chicken soup for the repressed soul.

"It doesn't matter who you are,

It doesn't matter who you are"

Toni belts higher and higher as the music swells, when another ensemble member grabs Dorian's head, breaking our kiss, and pulls him toward her.

Jenny, you bitch!

I can't wait to laugh about this with her over our post-show whiskeys and then fling this sexual energy onto Cary in our NoHo condo.

"'Cause you can be who you want to be,

When you're heeeeeeeere"

The music pauses before she lands a smooth finish on the title.

*"In the middle of the night."**

Blackout. While the audience golf claps with raised eyebrows, we exit the stage silently, containing ourselves until we can explode with jokes and exclamations in the cramped dressing room during intermission.

After the show, some castmates and I spring down the seedy streets of Hollywood, gabbing non-stop to a bar to celebrate another day of paid debauchery, a.k.a. acting. We're a hot mess: sweaty, wild hair that's been pin curled under wigs, sticky bodies from dancing under stage lights, varying amounts of stage makeup, and full of the glee of having spent the last three hours on and off stage together.

Jenny, Adam, Julianna, Mia, and I grab drinks at a raucous, Old West-themed bar, then head upstairs and sprawl on some eclectic old-timey furniture in the corner. I rib Jenny for tearing Dorian away from me in the orgy scene, then we laugh about that show's near misses, like when Mia's zipper got caught during a quick change, and total misses, like when Julianna blanked on the choreo during a dance break.

After the show's post-mortem concludes, Jenny says, "I'm planning to hike Runyon tomorrow if anyone wants to come." With her long, brown, wavy hair, big chestnut eyes, and vintage light blue dress, she looks like Judy Garland.

"I can't tomorrow," Julianna says, taking a ladylike sip of Merlot with her pouty, full lips. "Maybe next time."

When she and Mia start talking, my eyes flash at Adam, my sinewy gay bestie who's always decked out in an all-black runway ensemble.

I lean in to him and whisper, "She's probably got past life regression therapy," and we snicker to ourselves.

When Julianna told us about her past lives one brunch (the time she was a male Chinese prisoner, an Egyptian laborer, etc.), we used our best acting to keep straight faces. It's funny how L.A. typically turns people woo woo, but L.A. took the woo woo right out of me.

"Maybe eventually in this life she'll be a good actress," Adam whispers back. I snort laugh, and choke on my whiskey. Being a liberal agnostic is the tits.

"Mia's in for Runyon, how about you two?" Jenny asks Adam and me.

"I'll be recovering from the weekend," Adam says, lying back luxuriously on his settee. Orgies are hard work.

"I would, but I'm driving up to Santa Barbara to see my parents tomorrow," I say.

"That's a long drive. Do you spend the night?" Mia says in her velvety voice, with her head cocked.

"God, no. I'm used to the drive, and spending the day with them is about all I can handle."

Pretending to be a conservative Christian virgin is quite the energy suck. But the vision of them meeting the real me is worse: shocked and troubled faces as they question where they went wrong, followed by anguished praying in tongues, then pleading with me to repent or be damned.

"Oh, well, have fun visiting them tomorrow," Mia says sweetly.

Adam laughs. "Good luck trying to pull off still being a virgin," he smirks before taking a judgy sip of his Old Fashioned. My eyes shoot him playful daggers.

"What?" Jenny says. "Your parents can't really think you're still a virgin. Don't they know about Cary?"

"They've met him a few times," I say, remembering those stressful lunches where I was terrified Cary would let slip something that would trigger them or vice versa. Keeping my double lives as separate as possible is just better for everybody.

"My parents still live in a 1950s dream world where people don't have sex until they're married," I shrug. "And they DO NOT know we live together."

The one time they braved the too-long-and-uncomfortable-for-them drive to L.A. was to check out the condo I bought after I became full-time at my theme park show. That morning, I replaced my worldly wall art with the crosses and angels they'd gifted me over the years and removed any signs of a live-in boyfriend while Cary laughed at me.

At the end of the night, we exit the bar and hug goodbye while the evening summer air reeks of urine and weed, the one drug I've braved only to fall right asleep. I bike past cars, tents, bar hoppers, and tourists on my way to the metro, hoping I don't encounter last night's creep, who followed me around the subway platform and said how beautiful I looked in my stage makeup.

Then, a memory pops into my head that fills me with shame. One of my high school teachers had us do an exercise where he would read various scenarios of a rape, and for each one, we students were supposed to stand on one side of the classroom if the victim had done something to deserve it and the other side if they didn't. One scenario was that the victim was dressed in a revealing, suggestive outfit, and given my church training, I marched to what I now know is the wrong side. "Men can't help themselves!" I was taught. The teacher's face revealed thinly veiled disappointment, but I thought I was doing the right thing.

How could I have ever betrayed the sisterhood?

The kinship I feel with the women in my world is a fierce intimacy I never felt for churchgoers. As I ride the train home to North Hollywood, other destructive sayings I parroted, like "she was asking for it," echo in my brain, and my shame turns to rage.

———

The next morning, I zoom past the slow pokes and zip around the accidents on the 101 all the way to my parents' retirement community, to make up for sleeping in too late. They just moved into a small apartment in the independent living wing, where room service and housekeeping ease my aging mother's responsibilities. There's an assisted living wing for when Dad's disability reaches that point.

The blazing sun pierces my dry eyeballs from last night's whiskeys, so I chug water all the way. As L.A. blurs into empty hillsides, the nagging feeling that I shouldn't be this comfortable being one person with my parents and another with everyone else sets in. I'm used to lying by omission to them, but now some of my changed beliefs are almost too important to keep to myself, as if my silence makes me complicit in their condemnation of my chosen family.

I wonder what it's like to be in an unreligious family. What do they even talk about?

My Prius, a required L.A. accessory, screeches into a guest spot, and I throw back my birth control pill. I was shocked when my parents endorsed my car's outstanding gas mileage, given that they sneer at anything pro-environment for being part of "the liberal agenda."

I walk by the lavish landscaping, enter the lobby that boasts a grand piano and chandelier, and make my way down a tan hallway with impressionist paintings of fruit. I politely pass slow-moving residents in walkers and scooters until I reach the last door on the left, take a deep breath, and knock.

Susan, you're 29 years old. You're a grown ass woman. You attend HOA meetings. You do your own taxes. Why do you regress into an anxious, people-pleasing child when you walk through this door?

"Come on in!" Mom sings.

Wearing a T-shirt and jeans, my hair in a ponytail, I enter smiling and find her, in a fuzzy pink sweater, stretchy black jeans, and chunky shoes, to my right in the tiny kitchen. At 72, her blonde hair is thinner but still teased and hairsprayed to the nines. Her makeup just creases more in the wrinkles around her eyes and mouth.

"Good to see you!" we say together as we hug, and I hear the slow, steady rhythm of Dad's cane-assisted walking as he approaches from his bedroom in the back.

Wreaths with fake pink flowers adorn the otherwise empty white walls, and recliners patiently wait for my parents to spend the afternoon in them. Books and scribbled-on legal pads cover every flat surface: the side tables by each recliner, the small breakfast table, and even the kitchen counter, which also has some crumpled Milano packages on it and welcome cards from other residents.

Before I can ask how she is, Mom grabs a thick book off the kitchen counter and hands it to me.

"Here, this is for you. It's important. Do you realize the Federal Reserve was cooked up on an island years ago by a bunch of elites so they can use the government to make money?"

"The Creature from Jekyll Island," I say, reading the cover. "Okay, thanks, Mom. Sounds interesting," I say, playing along.

"Hi, Susan," Dad says with a smile. He wears a blue button-down shirt and khakis, and his short hair is mostly gray now with specks of black. He looks more and more like his father as age spots multiply and darken all over his face and arms.

"Hi, Dad. So, how's everything here? Are you liking it?" I ask, taking a seat at the breakfast table while they cozy into their recliners. Dad's is the dark gray one to my left that has a mechanized lift for assisting him getting in and out, and Mom's is the tan one to my right.

"It's fine," Mom says. "Well, just wait till you read that book." The fire in her eyes re-ignites. "The corruption just knows no end," she says, shaking her head. "I mean, look at the president. He wasn't even born here. He has no right to be our president! But the Democrats don't care, ya know."

Speak up, Susan. Be brave!

She glares off to the side and mutters bitterly, "Bleeding heart liberals. Bra-burning feminazis."

If you only knew, Mom. I'm a feminist, but I never use the word because you've forever tainted it with your disgust.

"Mom," I say, swallowing hard, starting to sweat, "he did produce his birth certificate, ya know, that shows he was born in Hawaii."

"Oh, and you're going to believe some piece of paper they fabricated? Ha!" she scoffs. "There's a documentary you need to see, Susan: *Loose Change.* It's all about 9/11. We've been watching so many videos on YouTube from high-up people in the military coming forward now and exposing the truth. It was all planned to start a war over oil. It always comes down to money. Unbelievable."

What?

"Hm," I manage.

"You'll notice no one high up in government was near the Twin Towers or the Pentagon that day. Now that's suspicious," she spits. "I mean, when you think about it, there's no way real planes could ever fly that low in a city without being shot down. The buildings were all rigged with explosives."

"So, you're saying the footage of the planes going into the buildings was fake?" I ask.

"Yes! Of course! Of course, Hollywood can do that," she says with a don't-be-so-naïve whine. "The same video was sent to all the news stations, and they just did what they were told and ran it."

I can't believe what I'm hearing.

"But in such a huge city, don't you think so many people would have had eyes on that area that they would have spoken up if there were never any planes running into buildings?" I ask.

While I search for logical responses to her insinuations, I wish I'd gotten a heads-up about today's debate. I didn't know I'd be arguing devil's advocate for the mainstream narrative of 9/11. I was an oblivious high schooler then, and it was Mom who woke me up that morning and said through trembling lips, "I want to cry, but I won't. You should see what's happening on the news."

"Susan, it was chaos that day. Everyone just sees the news and believes it. Well, not us anymore," she says now, 13 years later.

"Hm. Well, that would be a horrific thing to do, to sacrifice so many lives, to justify a war," I say, trying to ride the line between diplomacy and highlighting how crazy that sounds.

"It wouldn't be the first time," she snaps. "FDR got a telegram about Pearl Harbor the day before it was bombed, and instead of evacuating the base, he let it happen. Going to war was the perfect way to get us out of the Depression, and his approval rating was in the toilet."

Well, this is…new.

"Just watch that documentary. You'll see," she adds.

"Okay," I say, relieved to have a button on that one but still reeling over what she said.

What do I know? Could she be on to something? Maybe I will watch that doc.

"Have you found a church around here that you like yet?" I ask.

"Oh, we aren't going anymore," she says, matter-of-factly.

Ha! I've been lying about going to church this whole time when it's apparently not mandatory anymore!

"Oh?" I say.

"Every church we've tried is a letdown. No one's on our level," she says, resigned.

"You are pretty advanced, Mom." My parents' expert-level understanding of the Bible makes talking to most Christians frustrating for them.

I guess we're both evolving out of church in our own ways.

"How's Cary?" Dad asks.

Fantastic since we ended a dry spell and had sex last night.

"He's well. He just shot a commercial for an energy company."

"He's still in an apartment in Studio City?" he asks with an odd look in his eyes.

Is that a knowing smirk?

"Yeah," I lie, averting mine. "His roommate Jason is in Hawaii now, and his other roommate Matt just got a new job."

At least the update on his former roommates is true.

"How are you doing, Dad?"

"Well, I'm-" he starts, then stops, remembering something. "Oh! I've got a book for you, too. Let me get it." He hits the button that begins the slow lifting of the seat that helps him get out of the recliner, but I don't have the patience for it.

"Dad, I'll go get it," I say, getting up. "Where is it?"

"On my desk. A book called *Spirit, Soul, and Body*." I walk back to his room, which is completely bare except for a plain bed and a large desk covered in computer hardware, books, and papers. This is where I get my minimalism from. I retrieve the book and return.

"Thanks, Dad," I say, looking it over. Then he launches into a long explanation of this book, which details the differences among the spirit, soul, and body.

Sounds like dreadfully boring Biblical minutia to me.

But he is downright high on these spiritual revelations, so I promise to read it and add it to my bag. Although I usually just skim enough to find a talking point or two to make it look like I read it, if it comes up.

"Speaking of our souls," I say, seizing an opportunity. "I'm just wondering…"

Breathe.

"…I think one of the hardest things to grapple with is hell. I mean, Mom, I know you loved your father, right? But he wasn't a Christian when he died, so isn't it hard to think of him being in hell? Even though he was a good person and a good father to you? Doesn't that make you sad?"

"No," she says matter-of-factly. "I don't think about it. People know they've got sin, and it's up to them to do something about it."

Well, fuck me.

A siren goes by, and Mom scrunches up her face and holds her ears.

"Are you still pretty sensitive to noise these days, Mom?"

Her face falls, eyelids droop, and suddenly, she looks ten years older.

"Yes," she sighs.

The energy she's had for discussing global problems disappears when it comes to discussing personal ones.

"And no matter how many doctors I see or medications I try, I can't get this running out of my legs."

The constant adrenaline in her thighs and calves started after my parents were broken into a few years ago while they were home. Petrified, they holed up in the farthest room in the house until the police arrived. They've moved three times since, and when Mom wanted to leave this place in another spontaneous, fearful fit, Dad put his foot down.

"Hey, Susan, have you heard of M.G.T.O.W.?" Dad says, breaking the silence with a laugh.

"Umm, no. Is that an acronym for something?"

"Apparently, it stands for Men Going Their Own Way," he says, chuckling. "I've been watching videos of these women talk about how frustrated they are that men won't have anything to do with them anymore. It's some sort of movement, I guess."

"Huh," I say, dumbfounded.

What on earth is that about?

At 5 pm, we head to the community's dining room to beat the dinner rush. Throughout the meal, residents meander by our table and say hello. Once they're out of earshot, my parents lean in and whisper their life stories to me in headline form:

"Retired doctor, lost his wife last year."

"Swears a lot, owned a dress shop."

"Activities director, getting a divorce."

After dinner, I drive back to L.A. With the moonlit Pacific on my right, my mind stews on a strange, new disconnection with my parents.

The Federal Reserve? 9/11? M.G.T.O.W.? Their religion has always made them suspicious of our godless government.

It's all connected! I think, at the risk of sounding like a conspiracy theorist, too. I kick myself, though, for not having convincing rebuttals and airtight facts at my fingertips. I'm an actor, not a political scientist.

I guess it's harmless, though, right? Entertaining conspiracy theories?

*Dorian's Descent By Chris Raymond & Marco Gomez – Copyright holder – Requiem Media Productions, LLC

CHAPTER 22
WHAT ON THE FLAT EARTH?

"THE POPULARITY of conspiracy theories is explained by people's desire to believe that there is some group of folks who know what they're doing."

    -Damon Knight

~29~

A few months later, I walk into my parents' apartment with a determined smile and hope that whatever phase Mom was in last time has passed. I stroll to their breakfast table, and just as my butt hits the chair, Mom points a finger in the air and declares, "The moon landing was fake!"

Guess not.

I stare at her wide-eyed with raised eyebrows while Dad, in black slacks and a blue button-down, watches her with a smile from his recliner.

"This YouTube video I watched made a great point: who's running the camera while they're walking on the moon? It's so obviously fake once you think about it! You can see the rest of the set reflected in their helmets!" Mom scoffs, an armchair detective literally raving about her findings from her armchair.

As usual, all the lamps in their tiny living room are on, creating quite the dazzle in her big, clear glasses.

"We just had to beat Russia at all costs, and it was all done in Hollywood. I watched a whole thing on how they used a green screen," she says, her eyes lighting up on 'green screen' like it's a technology only insiders like her know about.

"You know, I demonstrate how green screens work in my show, like every day," I say with a tinge of attitude, alluding to my job hosting a theme park show about special effects in movies. When Hollywood and the entertainment industry are implicated, it stings.

That's my world, Mom.

"Well, I've also read enough now to know who killed JFK," she continues, nodding knowingly.

My eyes glaze over. "Oh?"

"Jackie fired the gun. The angles of the blood spatter match up from her point of view. You can see it in the video! But it was Lyndon Johnson's idea, so he could be president! He used her jealousy over all the affairs to talk her into it. Lee Harvey Oswald was totally innocent. They made that poor man take the fall." She shakes her head, bouncing her stiff wall of short blonde hair back and forth.

What can I say with any authority about an event so far away from life and experience?

I look to Dad for some help here, but he's still relaxing in his recliner, watching her through his thick, black glasses, and grinning ear-to-ear.

How is he not bothered by this? Should I just sit back and smile, too?

"Well, I had a film audition last week that I was pretty excited about," I say, eager to change the subject. I mention the famous director's name, but my excitement fades when Dad snickers.

"Is he in the Illuminati, too, Dawn?" he interjects, seemingly excited to rile her up.

"Probably!" she fires back, and he laughs.

He LOVES this! What is wrong with him?

"All the Hollywood elites are," Mom continues. "So many Democrats, our president-"

"What?" I say, incredulously.

I will not let you get away with this one.

"Oh, there's proof that Obama is in the Illuminati," she retorts.

"Show me," I fire back.

"I'll pull up the clip right now." She tips her head back and peers through the bottom half of her glasses while her fingers click away on her laptop, which rests on a half-pillow, half-hard surface contraption that serves as her recliner desk. I pull my chair up next to her and notice she's got several strips of masking tape over the laptop's camera. I point to the tape.

"What's with the-"

"It prevents them from recording you," she says off-handedly.

The clutter of saved YouTube video icons on her desktop offends my minimalist sensibilities, and I feel justified when it takes her a while to find the right one.

Eventually, she selects a commentary video on a press event of President Obama's. He addresses the media in front of a blue background at a podium, then dramatic music drowns out his audio. The focus zooms in on his hands as he concludes with a familiar gesture: kissing two fingertips, then holding up what looks like a peace sign.

Mom sees red. "There it is! The Illuminati symbol! Why would he do that if he wasn't part of it?" she says, assured that this is her slam dunk.

"Mom, why would he be so blatant if he was associating with a secret group that would hurt his reputation? And this is just a cool move that I've seen rappers do in music videos. It doesn't mean anything more than that."

She rolls her eyes. Whoever dismisses something as normal

or neutral always looks the fool compared to someone who claims to really know what's going on. I'm also at an age disadvantage. She will always sound older and wiser, and I will always sound young and naïve. As the conspiracy theories multiply by the minute, my energy to combat them wanes along with hope that anything I say will make a difference.

I'd love to share about what I think is my interesting actor life in L.A., filled with quirky characters and fun with Cary, but all that seems woefully unimportant and uninteresting to you, Mom, with all the government secrets there are to uncover.

Mid-afternoon, I make up an excuse to leave early, and their faces fall.

"You're not staying for dinner?" Mom says, surprised, sitting up.

"No, I wish I could," I lie, grabbing my purse and standing up. If I sit in this uncomfortable reality-bending gridlock any longer, I'll lose it. Better to leave before I say something I'll regret.

"Oh, okay," she says softly, looking like a chastised child. The mood is low when we say our goodbyes. We desperately want to be on the same page, but we're not reading the same book.

"Don't forget to email us that you made it home safe and sound," Dad says, as usual, standing and leaning over his cane in the awkward way that helps him balance.

"I will," I say weakly as I exit. On the other side of the door, I exhale, but I'm not relieved.

To make the most of driving all the way to Santa Barbara from L.A. and having the rest of the day free, I go to a wine bar on the pier to unwind and let the hypnotic waves work their magic. Sitting alone on the wooden deck with a sauvignon blanc that smells of wet hay, while the fall breeze flaps my long blonde hair and skirt, I look out over the navy-blue water and try to let go of my frustration and helplessness.

Religious nuts are one thing. I've coped with our spiritual differences by avoiding conflict and, when necessary, feigning agreement.

Conspiracy nuts are another. They MUST talk about it until you're convinced. How do we maintain a loving relationship amidst so much disagreement?

The wine's crisp citrus notes turn into a thick burn in my throat. I watch a squabble of seagulls violently fight over crumbs in the center of the pier.

Remember the bigger picture, Susan. You're lucky to have parents at all and ones who love you. Have compassion.

Mom's never been the same since that break-in. Perhaps her fear of the world is so overwhelming that concrete narratives, however far-fetched, restore her sense of control. I close my eyes and breathe in the salty air.

Empathy in, negativity out.

I set my wine down, resolved.

Ultimately, we're talking about events and people that are far away from our day-to-day lives. Because of that, they're impossible to actually get to the bottom of, so why fight it? All Mom wants, all anybody wants, is to feel seen and heard. I will love her by listening.

How hard can that be?

CHAPTER 23
FLAT EARTH WARMING

"NATION REELS After Gunman Massacres 20 Children at School in Connecticut."
-*The New York Times*

~29~

"Sandy Hook was a hoax!" Mom exclaims with absolute certainty from her recliner, wearing a hot pink shirt and stretchy denim jeans, at our next visit.

I close my eyes and repeat my new mantra in my head.

I will love her by listening. I will love her by listening.

But the cacophony of ticking from the multiple clocks in their small living room, one on every wall, scrambles my focus and adds to my aggravation.

Their hearing must be going.

"Well, first of all, you know the difference between a hoax and a false flag, right, Susan?" she says in a condescending tone.

Dad relaxes in his recliner, apparently enjoying the show.

"I don't think I do," I say, slow and controlled, my right leg bouncing with tension.

"Hoaxes are entirely fake. Nothing happened at all," she says with a big eye roll, throwing her hands in the air. "False flags actually happened, with real victims and all that, but one group sets it up to make it look like someone else did it."

My jaw tightens, and my eyes narrow.

"No one died in Sandy Hook," she continues. "They just found some very melodramatic crisis actors to play parents and teachers. There was a post on Craigslist for actors for it. A post, Susan! They found a mentally unstable guy to pin it on, Adam Lanza, and that was that."

"So, what is the agenda behind all these shootings then?" I ask, my voice strained.

I'm so inundated with counter-narratives to events I thought I knew that I honestly don't know what to believe anymore.

"Gun control, Susan!" she screams at me, angered by my ignorance. "They want to take our guns away! Then, when the American people are defenseless, that's when the Democrats can take over! But we won't let that happen, will we?" Mom says, shooting a fiery look at Dad.

"We sure won't!" he laughs from his recliner. His elevated feet in thick black sneakers practically tap together with enthusiasm.

He finds her eccentricities adorable instead of alarming. Why can't I see them that way?

While she continues ranting, I lose my grip on my mantra.

Don't take the bait, Susan. Just let her talk, stay quiet, and listen. It's pointless to-

"Mom, it's hard to believe every single shooting is some secret government operative," I blurt out. "I mean, they're not accomplishing anything toward gun control if they are. Sometimes there is just a crazy person with a gun, right?" I plead, desperate for common ground.

Mom looks at me the way I must be looking at her: utterly confused. She shrugs, then shakes her head, indicating "no" with a look of pity for how duped I am by the mainstream media.

No? That's not even possible?

Her absolute certainty and confidence knock me down like a giant wave. I can feel the strong hold my parents still have over me, the one that kept me a Christian long after I really was, when a small, little girl's voice in my head wonders:

Could she be right? What if everything I thought was true is a lie?

I slow my words down, so I don't lose it.

"All that's being pushed for now is a ban on assault rifles, weapons that are only for mass killing, Mom, not all guns. Why would anybody need that type of gun?" It's an honest question, not a regurgitation of a party line.

"Well, that seems reasonable…" she says, pausing to take this apparently new information in, then looking over at Dad, who's processing it, too. Whatever they're watching and reading obviously doesn't include this nuance.

I blink at them, astonished to have finally gotten through.

"…but that's just where they're starting!" she continues, fired up all over again.

I take a breath and summon the line I rehearsed for our next moment of impasse.

"Well, there's probably plenty happening that we're not informed of. I just hope you're vetting your sources for credibility."

I can see in Mom's eyes exactly what she's thinking: "YOU need to vet YOUR sources, Susan!" With pursed lips and fiery pupils, she stares at me with her arms folded.

I'm so tired of this. Get me out of here.

"How about we go for a drive?" I say.

She lights up. "Oh, sure!"

Dad gets into his red scooter to cover the long distance from their apartment to the car. We pile in, and I drive us by their favorite spots: the sprawling, equestrian estates of Hope Ranch, McDonald's for an iced vanilla latte, and finally, a park on a cliff overlooking the ocean where we watch sun-kissed college students jog by and middle-aged couples walk their dogs.

Dad stays in the car while Mom and I walk to the fence and enjoy the view on this surprisingly hot December day.

And climate change isn't real either, huh?

She gets out her Jitterbug cell phone, which is designed for seniors with basic features, large buttons, and yes or no prompts, and starts taking pixelated photos of the water with its rudimentary camera. When I raise my iPhone to take a photo of us, she whips her head away and puts her hand up.

"No, no, no, no, no," she protests.

"Mom! I don't have any photos of us!" I plead through giggles.

"No! They're not going to get *my* face," she says, laughing but determined.

I snap the pic.

CHAPTER 24
THE DAY THE EARTH WENT FLAT

"CHERISH those who seek the truth, but beware of those who find it."

-Voltaire

~30~

What on earth will we talk about today? I wonder on my way to visit my parents, as I speed past the picturesque California spring landscape: bright green hills bursting with yellow and purple flowers. Soon, the searing summer heat will dry everything out, leaving dusty cliffs and only the hardiest bushes.

Fresh energy pulses through me. Last visit's tension has had time to dissipate, so I return, as usual, re-charged with the hope that no matter what's thrown my way, I can handle it. When we last saw each other a month ago, Mom insisted I get off Facebook because it was funded by the CIA to spy on Americans. Then, when I confirmed that my iPhone has the Flashlight app, she was flabbergasted because...I have no idea.

In a casual, striped cotton dress, with air-dried wavy hair, I float from my car to their apartment door, yearning against all odds for a pleasant afternoon but braced for anything. In the long hallway leading to my parents' apartment, I pass a hunched-over woman inching along who smiles at me weakly, and a man whose long legs look cramped in his scooter.

Are they into conspiracy theories, too?

At my parents' brown door, a small shelf just to the right holds a card that shouts, "God bless!" After a centering deep breath, I knock.

"It's open!" Mom calls.

Keep it positive, Susan.

When I enter, she's characteristically all done up, beaming to see me, and wearing curve-hugging, belted black jeans and a shimmery gold turtleneck to cover the neck wrinkles she's self-conscious of. I hear the squeak of Dad's desk chair in his room as he gets up to join us.

"How was the drive?" she asks, standing next to the kitchen counter.

Oh, did my usual pep talk most of the way.

"Good! The Channel Islands were so clear today!" I gush. "And the spring flowers made the hillsides so beautiful. It was foggy and traffic-y until Ventura, then it all lifted, and the sun came out!" I say with a grin.

Mom takes a deep breath before speaking. Her face grows serious. "Well, Susan, you should know what we've just learned."

Here we go. You got this, Susan.

"The Earth is flat. We've been lied to our whole lives," she says, shaking her head. "Can you believe it?"

…

"It's true!" she continues, taking my slack-jawed, dumb-founded silence as a challenge to overcome. "And it starts in the schools! We're brainwashed from the very beginning. It's in text-books! I was taught all through school that the Earth is round, but if you just look out at the horizon, it's flat!" She laughs at how ridiculous it was to believe that the Earth was round in the first place.

...

While I struggle to form thoughts, my body slows everything down: my heart, my breathing, time. In a flash, this proclamation colors every fantastical one that came before it: the Rapture, healing, Ouija boards, Y2K, yoga, 9/11, the Illuminati…

It feels like the Earth is shifting under my feet, and I want to cry. I implicitly believed her for so long, and now I know I never should have. Everything till now has been somewhat, kind of, maybe, weirdly, miraculously possible, but I'm finally staring dead in the face the ONE thing I know, the one thing I'm absolutely sure of: the Earth is not flat.

Meanwhile, Mom is so energized by this revelation and all its implications that she beams like a lightbulb. Her bright eyes eagerly await my reply. With my throat dry, I carefully attempt a response.

"Now, Mom, I'm just trying to think through this," I say slowly, buying time. "You would want me to think through things and not just believe anything, right? That's what I'm doing."

I deserve the Nobel Peace Prize for diplomacy!

She purses her lips and shifts her weight back. That's not what she wanted to hear, but it's hard to argue with, which is my specialty these days. I desperately look to Dad, who leans on his cane on the other side of the kitchen counter and wears an indecipherable expression.

You, an educated, well-read, retired lawyer, can't possibly believe this, too?

"Susan, they're trying to control you." Mom jumps back in. "That's what they've been doing all along. What they get away with…" she mutters, looking off to the side.

"Um, who? Who is trying to control us by having us believe the Earth is flat?" I say, reaching for impossible words in an impossible conversation.

How do you politely break it to a loved one that they have lost their mind?

"The government! NASA is one big cover for running drugs. They're not exploring space, cause there is no space!"

I walk past her and collapse into a chair.

I need to be seated for this.

My purse falls from my limp shoulder to the carpet. The dam that contained my pain around my fractured relationship with my parents has finally burst. Disillusionment complete. Next step: anger?

My parents follow me to the living room and settle into their recliners. I notice the small tube TV they rarely used is gone, and I've been hearing less and less about dinners with other residents. My parents' world keeps getting smaller. And flatter, apparently.

"I'll show you what first tipped me off," she says, clicking away at her laptop on the half-pillow desk resting on her thighs. My eyes burn holes in Dad's face.

Speak up! Stop her! She'll listen to you!

But he keeps his head down and expression blank, pretending to be occupied with his lap or the splint that holds his paralyzed left arm.

"I came across a website that lists all these Bible verses that don't support a globe," she says, re-arranging the small pillows supporting her back while it loads. She peers through the bottom of her glasses and raises a finger to the screen to follow the text.

"Here we go. Isaiah 11:12: 'And he shall…gather the dispersed of Judah from the four corners of the Earth!' Genesis 1:7 says there's water above and below the Earth. It's all different from what we've been told!" Her eyes are full of giddy wonder over this new model.

Is she an adrenaline junky or something? She seems to thrive on daily revelations, and the bigger the better.

She continues reading verses that could be interpreted metaphorically, but of course, to her, every word of the Bible is not just true but literally true. To her, those verses can only mean that there are literally four earth corners and water is literally above and below us. This is what puts the 'fun' in fundamentalist Christian.

"Well, once I saw these verses, I found all these videos online and books about it, too!" she concludes.

"But-" I start.

Oh, why even try? When have you ever changed her mind?

I close my mouth and slump back into the seat.

No, you've GOT to, Susan!

I will myself to find the words.

"What about all the phenomena that support a sphere? Like day and night, seasons and time zones? All those fit with a globe revolving around the sun. If the Earth is flat, how is it sunny on one side and dark on the other?"

I've never felt more like a dumb actor than when I reach for facts from basic science classes a decade ago. Then again, I never thought I'd need to convince someone that the Earth isn't flat.

"That's just the way it works," she says, unfazed. "Susan, look at flight schedules. All the pilots are in on it. If you look at how long it takes to fly certain places, the flat earth model makes sense. People have checked flight times. I saw it."

What the fuck? Surely, flight schedules, of all things, can only support a globe model! Since we're just dismissing the obvious bits.

"So, if the Earth is flat-"

I can't believe I'm having this conversation.

"-it would be impossible to fly from LAX all the way over to New Zealand, right?"

I'm picturing a typical two-dimensional map of the Earth in my head with North and South America on the far left and Asia, Europe, and Australia on the far right.

"But there are flights there, I've actually been looking-" I say until she interrupts me.

"No, the longest flight is Australia to Argentina, because

those are the farthest apart on Earth." She looks at me with her head cocked.

"What?" I say sharply, visibly frustrated now.

With my blood pressure rising, I explain the map of the flat earth I'm envisioning, and she corrects me: the North Pole is the center of the world. Picture a globe, then press the top of it down until the continents are swirling in a flat circle around the North Pole.

Flabbergasted, I point to how the hot equator and freezing north and south poles make sense on a sphere relative to the sun.

I then try to glean specifics about the dark purpose behind such a massive lie that involves so many people, to which she admits, unconcerned, that she doesn't have answers for everything yet. But that alone only makes her more excited. Her whole body is invigorated by this new revelation from scripture. She's committed to learning everything there is to discover and fighting for the truth to come out. As the minutes grow, though, so does her annoyance with my resistance. She wants me on board the flat earth train just as much as I want her off of it.

"I'm going to need some time with this one. Okay?" I say, finally, to hold her off.

Her light dims. I'm not just rejecting a belief. I'm rejecting her. This is the impossible tightrope I've walked my whole life that keeps my innards in knots.

How can I be myself without hurting you, Mom?

I look to Dad one last time to inject some level-headedness into this insanity, but his eyes won't meet mine.

"Well, I'll send you these verses so you have them," Mom says, whipping up an email to me on her laptop with a few loud clicks of her acrylic nails.

I watch her while smoke comes out of my ears.

Mom, I can pretend to still be a Christian.

I can conjecture with you about who killed JFK.

But I CANNOT entertain for ONE SINGLE FUCKING SECOND that the Earth is flat.

I change the subject to an upcoming trip for a friend's wedding, but in my head, there's a needle stuck in a record's groove making me nauseous and repeating, "The Earth is flat, the Earth is flat, the Earth is flat…"

When we go for a drive late afternoon and end up at Mom's favorite ocean-view park on the bluff, she looks out over the horizon and mutters to herself, "See? It's flat. You can see it!"

"Mm," I say.

I HAVE to put a stop to this one. Not just for her sake but for mine.

At the end of the visit, I stumble to my car in a daze and fall into the driver's seat. The emotions I've been suppressing for the sake of pleasantries bubble to the surface as the 30-year-in-the-making image of my mother, and therefore myself, irreversibly unravels. Flat earthers are the most globally laughed at group of idiots, and lumping her, my dear, misguided mother, in with them hurts. I want to protect her from the mean kids on the playground.

Am I somehow responsible for this? Should I have spoken up earlier and stronger in her conspiracy journey? If I had given her grandchildren to be occupied with or connected my worlds better by bringing friends around, would she have stayed more grounded in reality and not had time to be brainwashed? Is she just tragically gullible? Does this make her feel important?

My adulthood has been a fast-as-you-can sprint away from everything my parents built my childhood around, but my Pollyanna heart foolishly thought we could stay the close-knit family we once were. Our ideological distance doesn't undo the fundamental tether created by the countless, foundational hours we've spent together. There's still a kid inside me who wants to leave the thinking and the choices to the adults in the room, but not these adults. Not anymore.

What will put me over the edge of the Earth is if Dad goes along with this one. I've been wary of Mom's judgment since I was a teen, but I've always respected his thoughtfulness and reasoning, even when he'd warn me every few years about an imminent financial collapse that would usher in the End Times.

Oh, god, why did I ever believe anything either of them said?

I call Cary on the way home and vent.

Luckily, though, I have an idea.

The Bible got us into this mess, but the Bible can get us out of it.

CHAPTER 25
STOP THE FLAT EARTH,
I WANT TO GET OFF

"FAITH...IS the art of holding on to things your reason has once accepted, in spite of your changing moods."
  -C.S. Lewis

~30~

When I get home from the most insane conversation I've ever had with my parents, and that's saying something, I blow past Cary watching *Avengers* for the millionth time and race to my laptop in our room. I always email my parents to say that I got home safely, but tonight, I've got something to add.

I HAVE to prove to her that the Earth isn't flat before she gets entrenched.

My fingers furiously type "Bible verses about a round earth" into the Google search bar while I sit cross-legged on our blue and green striped comforter. Any links I send from mainstream science or media, Mom will reject, but scripture she'll have to reckon with. Surrounding me are colorful framed vacation photos (my side) and comedic posters of stormtroopers smelling daisies (Cary's).

On my drive home, my mind dredged up a Sunday school

lesson from my childhood that I hadn't thought about in years. Miss Henning, a thin, pale, redheaded young woman in a floral dress, said in her high-pitched voice, "Long ago, when most people believed the Earth was flat, it was the Christians who knew it was round based on verses in the Bible!" She glowed with pride. "This is another way we know we can trust in the Word of God! He shared the inner workings of the universe with us before man figured out any of it!"

My, how we've come full circle.

My eyes frantically search the results and flash on a web page that lists all the Bible verses that relate to the shape of the Earth, so I click on it. The top line: "Isaiah 40:22: 'It is he that sitteth upon the *circle* of the Earth.'"

Boom! There it is! Score one for the Bible!

This webpage even includes the verses Mom cited but interprets them as compatible with the sphere thanks to deep dives into theology, context, and the original Greek! The internet giveth all things one seeketh.

I compose an email to my parents: "I made it home safe," blah, blah, blah, "good to see you today," etc., etc., "oh, and here are some Bible verses that support the scientifically-proven shape of the Earth." I hit 'Send' and stare at the screen for a moment.

Hm.

Feeling suspicious, I Google "did Christians believe the Earth was round when everyone else believed it was flat?"

One of the top articles is about the myth that Columbus discovered America while trying to prove the Earth is round. I scroll down and read:

"It's almost certain that in the 1490s, nobody thought the Earth was flat...no educated person in the history of Western Civilization from the third century B.C. onward believed that the Earth was flat."

Ouch.

Sunday school was wrong again.

The next day, I frequently check my email for her reply. Nothing.

———

I chew on my lip as I approach my parents' apartment a month later, hopeful but nervous. Mom never replied to my email.

Maybe she's embarrassed she fell for something so absurd that she doesn't want to acknowledge it ever again? I can do that. Happily.

I knock our signature knock and shift my weight back and forth to release my nervous energy.

"Come on in!" she hollers.

I enter and am instantly taken aback. Mom, in a collared red shirt, jeggings, and a chunky necklace, looks noticeably thinner.

"Well, look at you, Mom!"

"Oh, yeah?" she says with a smile on her matching red lips. She puts her hands on her hips and turns this way and that, showing off all 5'5" of her. She's a classic pear: petite torso with pillow-like legs, but she's down a size or two at least. It's the thinnest I've ever seen her.

"Cabbage soup diet!" she says with a snap. "Easy, tasty, I can do it. I make a big batch, and that's one of my meals every day, sometimes two!"

"Well, that's great, Mom! I'm so happy for you!" I say, clapping while she does another 360. Weight Watchers, Jenny Craig, and Atkins made her so miserable that Dad and I were always relieved when she'd quit. If he accompanies her to a doctor's appointment, she makes him look away when she steps on the scale.

Dad joins us, and we all take a seat in their narrow, neutral-toned living room: white walls, tan carpet, dark wood furniture. The hazy SoCal sun filters in through the white vertical blinds that cover the sliding door to their small patio.

"Delivery!" a man's voice hollers as he knocks on their front door.

"I'll get it," I say, standing. I open the door, take a heavy box from a stocky young man, and set it on their white kitchen counter. "Want me to open it?"

"Yes! Those are my new science books about the flat earth!" she says, excitedly.

Oh.

Guess she didn't care for my verses.

"Oh, okay," I say, deflated, getting scissors out of the drawer and opening the box. Inside are three thick books that I instantly judge based on their pixelated, low-resolution cover graphics. One has generic math equations all over it.

"Let me see!" she calls, so I bring them over to her. "I can't wait to read these! People have really proven it's flat!" she beams.

"Mm." I fall back into my chair, hopes dashed. "Mom, did you look at those Bible verses I emailed you?"

Her head pops up after being buried in the books. "Huh?"

"I emailed you those Bible verses that indicate that the Earth is round. And that web page addressed the verses you told me about last time, too. Those didn't resonate with you at all?"

She has no idea how much rides on this.

She thinks for a moment, like she's trying to remember something from long ago.

"Well, no," she says softly with doe eyes. "This is the way it is." She holds up one of the books and says, "The Earth is flat."

Well, fuck me up the Earth's ass.

A wall goes up around my heart.

"And ya know, now when I think about all those rocket launches from Vandenberg-" she says, revving up and referencing the air force base Dad worked at, "-all one big show. Phony baloney!"

I look at Dad sitting across from me at the table, his short gray hair so thin that I can see sunspots on his scalp. He watches her with a blissful smile, somehow at peace with all this nonsense.

Are you going to let her get away with saying your work was point-less? Irrelevant? Fake? Seriously?

"I'll be right back," Mom says, putting the books on the side table and awkwardly scooting out of her recliner. "The only downside to eating cabbage soup all the time," she laughs on her way to the bathroom.

Perfect timing.

I've been dying to talk to Dad alone. I lean over the table toward him when I hear the bathroom door close.

"Dad," I say, in a hushed voice with pleading eyes. "Please tell me you don't think the Earth is flat."

How are these words I'm actually saying in my real life?

"There could be something to it. There's a lot out there about it," he says, gesturing to the books, then to the walls.

That's when I notice them: two flat earth posters Scotch taped at eye level, a small black and white one in the kitchen, and a medium-sized color one in the living room. Seeing them knocks the wind out of me.

It's over.

My parents are fools.

How long before I lose my marbles?

I take a deep breath and address him stronger than I ever have, bucking the ingrained submissive "honor your father and mother" bit.

"Dad, the Earth is not flat," I say through gritted teeth.

How can I get this through to you? Don't you know what's at stake?

I've maintained a rosy, no-judgment openness to religion as part of my agnosticism, because it's too painful to look back at my childhood and think that everyone I was surrounded by was duped. And who am I to comment on religions I know very little about?

But with Christian-turned-flat-earther parents, I can't help but think that the devoutly religious are like I was, brainwashed from a young age, or gravitating to whatever eases their adult existential anxiety, unable to face the cold, harsh reality that there is no rhyme or reason to anything, and nothing happens after we die.

Is religion the original conspiracy theory?

The cacophony of clocks interrupts my thoughts and jolts me back into the room, and my statement to my father, that the Earth is not flat, hangs in the air. With each ticking second, I feel my upbeat "oh, I don't know, I'm open!" stance on religion being replaced by an angry "it's insane to be anything but an atheist."

Dad looks at me sheepishly, like he knows that he's going along with something he shouldn't, but what else can he do? Not only does he love her, but as an invalid, he needs her.

"It's not really of consequence to me whether it's flat or round," he says with a shrug. "The Word, Susan, being in the Word, living in the Word, that's..." His voice trails off as he shakes his head, and his eyes moisten. The Bible means so much to him.

"Oh, did you read that book I gave you yet? *Spirit, Soul, and Body*?" he says.

Busted.

"Not yet, Dad. Sorry."

Why would I read anything you recommend now?

When Mom returns, she picks up right where we left off.

"Well, Susan, there is a whole flat earth community, it turns out! There's the society, message boards, and people who go on talk shows and expose the truth. It's really something!"

As she expands on the online flat earth world, I notice something.

Is she happy?

Instead of crabbily raving about cover-ups, she looks thrilled to have found like-minded people.

Everyone needs community. This, of all places, is where she fits in now. I guess I'm happy for her?

When I get home that night, I see an email from her with links to more flat earth "proof." In our living room with hardwood floors, a popcorn ceiling, and movie posters on pale green walls, I slump next to Cary on our L-shaped salmon couch and show him her email. He shakes his head and reaches for the remote. I stare at the email while he resumes our Netflix binge of *Lost*.

Time to be direct.

"Mom," I type. "Respectfully, this is one we have to agree to disagree on. I want our time together to be pleasant, and any more discussion about this is going to be unproductive."

I hit 'Send' and feel positively drunk with power over laying down a boundary.

Why haven't I done this before?

CHAPTER 26
FLAT LITTLE EARTHERS

"NEVER WORK WITH ANIMALS OR CHILDREN."
 - W.C. Fields

~31~

I walk to set from hair and makeup, escorted by an eager, young production assistant, repeating my three lines under my breath with my blonde hair perfectly straightened. In a casual teal top and capri tan slacks, I look the part of a mom for this mommy and me class scene in a network comedy.

"Okay, ladies, are any of you actually moms?" the assistant director asks us, wearing a ballcap, his face unshaven.

I shake my head "no," as do my fellow actors with lines in the scene: a tall, bony brunette and an amiable young black woman with handfuls of tight curls at her shoulders. They're also in colorful mom attire.

"All righty then. Baby class for all of you before we rehearse." He points to our right, where a nurse and a stable of actual moms holding their infants stand in what looks like a soundproof glass enclosure. They wave at us wearily, but their eyes match our excitement to be on set today. In loose clothes, with their pale faces framed by wispy, stray hairs, the real moms look nothing like us, the TV moms.

We're holding real babies for the scene? No! I assumed we'd be holding dolls!

"Oh, great!" I say with a big smile as we walk toward them.

I avoid holding babies like they're grenades.

You made this, this is your problem, what are you handing it to me for? I think when someone asks if I want to hold one.

Whether it's narcissism, selfishness, a childhood spent mostly around adults, or just a cold, dead heart, I have never wanted to be a mother. Nothing is more precious to me than my freedom. Explaining this to puzzled faces is tiring: "I just don't want them, okay? I'm never babysitting Xander, sorry."

My co-stars and I walk into the room with the nurse and real moms. Half the babies are wailing.

Hey, kiddos, I had an early ass call time, too, but you don't see me crying.

The nurse talks us through baby holding etiquette, like supporting the neck at all times. Then we actors are each handed a baby, told its name, and given personalized tips.

"Leonard loves when you sing to him!" his mom chirps at me.

"Ooo!" I squeal while stiffly holding her smelly offspring. Most of my acting today is happening now. I look down at this foreign, strange thing with a plastered smile on my face.

Sorry, Leonard, I only sing for paying customers.

He's light at least and sound asleep, miraculously unfazed by my boiling blood that resents this expectation of woman-hood. Meanwhile, the other actors fawn over their new little besties, as females are supposed to do, and bring up their adorable nieces and nephews, relatives I don't have as an only child.

"Wahhhhhhhhh! Wah wah waaaaaahhhhhhh!" Leonard screams out of nowhere, like a demon rising from the dead. His piercing cries rile up the others, and I quickly hand him back.

How can we film anything with bawling babies? This is going to take forever!

"Okay, time for rehearsal!" the A.D. says, popping in.

He walks us back to set, a small colorful playroom with eight pillows in a circle. The principal actors sit on two of the pillows and appear deep in conversation. The characters they play have babies now in season two, so they regularly work with a handful of infants.

What a pain in the ass.

I nail my lines during rehearsal sans-kiddos, but I'm anxious for when we film, resentful of the unpredictable obstacle that could ruin my preparation and timing.

"OK, lighting needs more time. You can relax, but be ready," the AD says.

I walk past the real moms, who are too absorbed in patting and petting their babies to see me waving at them.

As I step back into my shiny wood dressing room, I smile.

Having a trailer never gets old.

Seated at the vanity, I look into my blue eyes and relish the peaceful solitude of a room without kids.

Thank god my birth control pills have never failed me.

My worst fear, since becoming SEXUALLY ACTIVE, is seeing two lines on a stick after a tinkle. That would be my make-or-break moment: nonchalantly take the action I espouse as a liberal woman or succumb to my upbringing and be unable to stop what will be (is?) a life.

Early on, I figured I would have to have the baby I've never wanted and hide from my parents for nine months or fess up and face their judgment. Then I'd put it up for adoption, fucking my career, my body, and my soul. But at least god would be happy, right?

Then, while walking one morning from my condo to my car, the type of mindless routine movement that allows your brain to have a breakthrough, I had a revolutionary thought: *what if a woman's dreams for her life were allowed to be more important than a fetus?*

You're doing something wrong! You're doing something wrong!

That rang in my head the first few months Cary and I slept together.

You're going to be punished for this! You're going to be punished for this!

And I knew what my punishment would be. Cary wouldn't be punished, no. My belly would show the sin. I hate being a woman. I hate being vulnerable, dismissed, expected to be perfect, someone else's ejaculation away from getting pregnant, and paid less. Yes, even at my longtime theme park show, the highest-paid role is male-only.

I'm furious now at how many years I wasted being tied up in knots over sexuality, something some savor as life's peak pleasure. With my parents' judgment now completely out the window, I'm done being non-committal about anything they ever taught me, full stop. I am Angry. By the power of my free mind, I've shattered the heavy chains of religion's control, sexual and otherwise, which kept me bound, fearful, and anxious.

But I'm still too scared to open the vibrator I won at a benefit I danced in two years ago.

"All right, Susan, we're ready to shoot," a P.A. calls from outside the door.

"Coming! Thank you!"

I get to my mark on set and am handed an enormous, whimpering child named Samuel.

This sandbag is a newborn?

He's as heavy as a full grocery bag of liquids but squirmier. We do a take, and I am bouncing the kid so much to quiet him that the director tells me curtly, "Less."

I look down at my drooling co-star.

Don't fuck this up for me, Samuel.

We do another take, but three lines in, it's ruined by several babies crying. Eventually, they extract the loudest ones, including Samuel, and I could kiss the P.A. when he hands me a doll wrapped in a blue blanket. We do two flawless takes and cut.

"All right, that's a wrap on Susan, Mel, and Heather! Thank you!" the A.D. hollers, and everyone claps, as is custom.

We walk back to our trailers, exchanging social media handles, thrilled to have done the impossible: booked a legit acting job. Filming at Manhattan Beach Studios on a Friday at 31 years old, I am living my dream, and I shudder to think how easily my life could have gone another way.

CHAPTER 27
JOURNEY TO
THE CENTER OF
THE FLAT EARTH

"IT'S EASIER to fool people than to convince them that they have been fooled."

-Mark Twain

~31~

A week later, I'm still walking on clouds from my day on set when I enter my parents' apartment beaming in a floral summer dress. As soon as I walk in, I see Mom's giddy with gossip. Her blonde bouffant buzzes as we take our usual seats under the flat earth posters.

I just worked with some famous actors, Mom, but no, you first.

"So, you remember the flat earth YouTuber, Patricia Steere, right?" she says, grinning ear-to-ear, barely able to contain her excitement as she pulls on her recliner's wood lever to lift her feet.

"Patricia Steere," I say, remembering. "Yes, when we last left her, she was dating another flat earther. They go on shows together now like some flat earth power couple, right?"

One day, having flat earthers for parents rocks your whole

world. A month later, it's like your funny bone, just an odd part of life. A year later, I can't remember things any other way.

"Yes!" she exclaims. "She and Mark Sargent have had this whole public affair, but they've been fighting lately. They openly argue now when they go on shows together! Trouble in paradise!" she sings.

Mom doesn't push her flat earth belief on me anymore, shockingly respecting baby's first boundary, but it's likely because she's now far more absorbed by the reality show-level romances, alliances, and betrayals playing out on flat earth YouTube channels. And she can't keep all this juice to herself!

"Patricia's the one who flew to England to move in with her last boyfriend, right?" I add. "And he would hold up signs in the back of her videos that said, 'Help.'"

That was pretty funny.

Mom guffaws. "Yes! That was hilarious! My goodness! Well, everyone is up in arms now over Patricia because official property records were found and posted that show that her home in Texas was paid for by F.E.S." She drops the letters slowly and dramatically, ending with a gasp.

"F.E.S.," I repeat quizzically. I look at Dad, nodding off in his recliner. His eyes keep closing while his head rolls to the side before jerking back up.

Mom stares at me, bug-eyed, waiting for a reaction. As ever, I'm at a loss.

"Everyone's thinking that must stand for Flat Earth Society!" she bursts. "Now what can that mean?"

Oh! I know!

"Mom, they may be paying her. Maybe her house is really a studio of sorts for her to film content." I explain to her what an influencer is: someone paid to promote something on their social media. Hope rises in me that this could be Mom's way out.

Oh my god. What if the Flat Earth Society is the actual conspiracy?

Mom blinks at me blankly. To her, I'm not making any sense, but for me, it's all coming together.

The curtain's pulled back! We're looking at the Wizard of Oz!

"You know, Mom, drama like Mark and Patricia's romance and lovers' quarrels is great for driving views and selling ads and making revenue, just like the spreading of outrageous theories is. It's so eye-catching, it gets clicked on and makes people money. The people with followings because of this, like Patricia and Mark, may not believe any of this stuff at all. They could just be getting paid."

It's all a sham, Mom! Don't you see?

She chews her lip, and with eyebrows furrowed, she looks at me like I'm speaking Greek. Like her religion, her worldview is set. No amount of proof, or lack of, could convince her otherwise.

Mom now woefully resembles her mother, Grandma Spencer, who couldn't be swayed from believing the tabloids (or 'rags' as Mom called them) that she devoured weekly at the beauty parlor (or 'booty party' as I called it as a kid). When Mom would scold her for falling for a headline about a snake with a human head found in Wyoming, Grandma would defend herself with a terse, "How can they print it if it's not true?"

Does this run in my family? Will a switch turn on in my brain at some point that makes me believe everything I read? Sounds like a Jim Carrey movie.

"Well, I don't know what it all means, but it sure is interesting!" Mom concludes, just as titillated as when she began.

Maybe The Truth isn't as important to her as she says it is? Maybe the wild world wide web just makes life interesting.

"How are you doing, Dad?" I say, moving on.

In loose tan pants and the one light pink collared shirt Mom got him to "brighten up his wardrobe," he looks at me with droopy eyes and a half smile.

"Oh, I'm all right. I'm working on fixing my digestion with some new supplements. I always take my echinacea with goldenseal root and gingko biloba, but now I'm doing fish oil and niacin," he says proudly. "That reminds me, I have a book on niacin and a bottle of some for you before you go. It reduces inflammation."

"Thanks, Dad."

What can you do when someone is so misguidedly kind?

"Good health starts in the gut, Susan!" he says with a smile and an index finger in the air. He elaborates about the online sleep seminars he's watching for his chronic insomnia, and I bite my tongue.

When I found out he pays for them and saw the sensational emails they send him ("Get better SLEEP TONIGHT!!! THE NEVER BEFORE HEARD 10 tips doctors AREN'T telling you!!!! ONLY $49.99!!!!!), I warned him it might be a scam. Clearly, that didn't land.

"I hope it helps, Dad," I say, resigned.

Our roles have reversed. As much as I want to protect my parents from the world, they're old enough to make their own decisions.

"Well, I had a fun day on set last week!" I say, launching into the details, complete with asides about my infant co-stars. "There's just nothing like the high of booking a TV show," I swoon.

This was my fourth. Signing with a new manager finally elevated my career to this level.

"Getting the call that in all of Los Angeles, I got it! Hundreds were submitted by agents and managers, they auditioned maybe 20 or 30, called back a few, and then they picked me!"

As an actor, you're usually too something: too short, too tall, too fat, too thin, too young, too old, too pretty, too average. Getting the call means that, for once, you are perfect. "It's the best feeling in the world!" I say with a grin.

"Well, you've never had a baby," Mom quickly chides with a twinkle in her eye that sparkles through her big, clear glasses.

I guess my thing doesn't compare to your thing.

Then I'm stunned when she bursts into tears.

"Having you was the most wonderful thing that ever

happened to me!" she sobs. Tears stream down her cheeks, creating glistening lines in her blush before falling onto her fuzzy white turtleneck sweater.

"Oh, Mom," I manage, leaning towards her.

My brain fixates on our aggravating differences, but in between the difficult conversations are her warm check-in emails, the way she responds enthusiastically to every detail in my replies, and an embarrassing number of thoughtful gifts.

"It was!" she continues. "It just didn't seem like life was going to go that way, but then you came along!"

I was a surprise delivery five years into my parents' marriage.

"Grandma got the shock of her life when I called to tell her I was pregnant. At 42 years old! Ha! I'll never forget it. She just kept saying, 'What?'" Mom imitates Grandma, repeating "What?" with different line readings: shock, disbelief, thrill.

"You-" Mom sniffles and looks me in the eyes. "-changed my life."

The room warms and fades to soft focus. The negativity I harbor about my mother turns to guilt over all the times I've been exasperated with her beliefs. What a nasty way to treat someone who loves me SO much. Instead of getting the warm fuzzies, as she intends, her profound declaration makes me feel undeserving and overwhelmed.

You didn't condition me for grand displays of affection, Mom!

I struggle to respond while Mom grabs a Kleenex and dabs her eyes. Dad snores in his recliner.

Must change the subject. Big feelings hard.

"Have you heard of tiny homes, Mom?" I say, my voice cracking, hoping I'm not inadvertently triggering a conspiracy theory with the new topic. You never know.

"I think they're so cool. I mean, they're so affordable and efficient, and I love the gorgeous settings people have them."

"I've seen those. They are fascinating!" Mom says. "They're

all so different!" She starts pulling up some of her favorites on her laptop while Dad's eyes wearily open.

"What? What's all different?" he says.

"Tiny homes, Dad, ever heard of them?"

"Oh, tiny homes," he repeats in a sleepy daze. Then the words register, and he awakens fully. "They can be off-grid, right? They're all over the prepper websites I follow," he says, still anticipating an imminent global financial collapse.

Once, when I described an L.A. neighborhood as "preppy" to him, he got excited, thinking there were preppers there. I clarified, "Clean cut, Dad, not doomsday."

Well, stop everything. Do we actually agree on something? The stars align just this once every 100 years. Brigadoon has come to life!

Tiny homes, of all things, are the sole items in our Venn diagram of shared interests. We spend the rest of the afternoon until 4:30 pm dinner comparing photos and videos of quirky miniature houses in scenic, serene locations. It's my happiest parental visit in ages. Precious few parts of our core selves connect anymore.

I'm the one who changed, not them. I did this to us. I have to forgive myself for that.

CHAPTER 28

THE EARTH IS FLAT...AND SO AM I

"CONSPIRACY THEORY IS the ultimate refuge of the powerless. If you cannot change your own life, it must be that some greater force controls the world."

-Roger Cohen

~32~

"My girlfriend was there. She called me while she was running for her life to tell me that she loved me," the middle-aged Hispanic man says to me with traumatized eyes. The dim lighting in the lobby of this old black box theatre in Hollywood makes the small crowd look like shadows milling about. Fractured light from a streetlamp outside illuminates his emotional eyes.

The mass shooting at the Mandalay Bay hotel in Las Vegas during a country music festival has dominated the news and conversations for the last few weeks.

"Oh," I say from behind the box office, putting a hand over my mouth. I'm helping a friend who organized tonight's play reading by handling tickets. "I hope she's okay."

He nods. "I was worried all night. She didn't call again until about noon the next day. She said she just kept running, she and a small group around her. They kept having to jump over barriers, and she was in stilettos. They just kept running…" He looks down.

An older couple approaches the box office from behind him, so he nods politely back at them and moves to the side so they can get their tickets from me.

"Well, I'm so glad she's okay. Enjoy the reading," I say to him.

While I check the couple off the list and hand them programs, I can't get the vision of a terrified woman jumping hurdles in stilettos in the Vegas night out of my mind.

Cary and I know a couple who were there, too: his best friend's cousin and her husband. They survived, but the couple they went with did not. Reading their Facebook post was a gut punch, and we heard they've started therapy.

My rage and heartache over this too-close-to-home event do not portend well for my visit with my parents tomorrow.

Last year, when a mass shooter killed 49 people at the Pulse nightclub in Florida, I could barely contain my tears while performing my theme park show, where a number of my co-workers have Orlando connections.

Then I could barely contain my frustration when Mom ranted about it all being phony baloney, just another lie perpetuated by the mainstream media, so Democrats could disarm the American people.

Just try, Mom. Tell me this one's a hoax, too. I fucking DARE you.

———

After an unusually gray, miserable, drizzly drive up from L.A., I walk into my parents' apartment the next day, my pink raincoat and brown boots dripping, and hope this visit doesn't go sideways. The flat earth posters immediately bring me down to… well, Earth.

After bemoaning the infuriating two-and-half-hour, bumper-to-bumper crawl up the 101 in the rain, I fall into my usual chair. Mom does the same, and as soon as her butt hits the recliner, she starts in.

"This Vegas thing didn't happen, you know, Susan. It's a hoax!" Mom spits, perturbed.

My nostrils flare, and I breathe deeply. Light rain raps their sliding glass door, and the overcast weather dims the room and mutes the mood.

Dad sits across from me at the small breakfast table, hunched over the large white tray that holds his pills. With his one working hand, he's carefully filling his clear weekly pill case with a few prescriptions and many alleged cure-all supplements and vitamins. His routine preoccupation with touching the bottles, rearranging them, and reading the labels feels obsessive, likely born from the need to regain control over his health after his stroke.

"The video of the man claiming to be an eyewitness is so unbelievable, and it's all they've got!" Mom continues. "It's so obvious that the MSM (mainstream media) is just airing what they're given without checking anything because they're saying the same script! It's all fake!"

She's so worked up, I fear she'll tip the recliner and fall backwards.

"It's just like when they all said Hillary-" She says the name with a snarl. "-won the popular vote. No, she didn't!"

Dad looks up from his pills.

"Yes, she did, Dawn."

"She did?"

"Yes."

"Oh." Mom backs down.

THAT'S where you draw the line, Dad?

"Well, Hillary runs a-" Mom stops herself from saying the vile word full volume. "-pedophile ring, Susan," she whispers, horrified.

I close my eyes and stifle a facepalm. Mom's inflamed eyes, as red as her turtleneck and lipstick, await my reply.

"Mom, sometimes an event simply happens at 5 pm with 100 people in Washington, D.C., and every news station is going to say that because those are the facts! Different media reporting the same details doesn't necessarily mean that it's all rigged. Maybe, just maybe, it's proof that we can be pretty sure a thing happened!"

"That's not what I'm talking about, Susan," she says, exasperated, her short blonde hair shaking. "Not mundane events. I'm talking about these big lies like a shooting with fake footage and crisis actors and a set-up suspect, who, of course, shoots himself right after. Sooooo convenient, puh-lease!" She rolls her eyes. Her smug vitriol is the stick that stokes my embers.

"Mom, I have friends who were there! The couple they went with died! My friends are in therapy now to deal with everything they went through!"

Surely, THAT will shut you up!

She hesitates, then says, "Did you know this other couple? The couple who died?"

You're calling my friends liars, now? Wow, conspiracy theorists will stop at nothing to debunk whatever contradicts their narrative.

"No, but I have no reason not to believe my friends. Cary and I have been going to their parties for, like, eight years now. They're posting on Facebook about it. They were posting about being at the festival days before the shooting, because they're big country music fans. I met a guy last night whose girlfriend was there. She called to tell him she loved him while she was running for her life. This involves so many people, Mom. How can you think this is made up?"

Silently, she dives into her laptop, pulling up the "unbelievable eyewitness" clip she saw. She turns the computer to face me and hits 'Play.'

A scatter-brained man in a plaid fedora at a nondescript location at night rambles about a shooting under a bright camera light. No respectable news outlet is running this.

So, this is how the suspicious are radicalized. Since they're making a point to not watch any mainstream news, anything can be passed off as "all over the news!" No wonder they can't believe the general public buys it. I could wring the necks of the conscienceless swine responsible for the glut of sham content brainwashing my parents. Wring. Their. Necks!

"Mom, no one is airing this obviously fake video!"

Then I whip out my iPhone. Our devices are the weapons for this battle, apropos since modern conflict is often what I see on my technology box versus what you see on yours. I pull up news stories with various footage, interviews, and investigation details, and show them to her in desperation, but she's uninterested. She shakes her head at me slowly with a look of pity for how controlled I am.

The embers in my chest burst into flame. My voice screeches out at a raw pitch I've never heard before, vibrating with intensity.

"Mom, I don't know how to handle this!" I scream. "It is so hard to come here month after month and deal with the fact that everything I know is happening in the world you tell me is not! My friends are saying they've lived through a horrible tragedy, which I have a lot of compassion for. And then I come here, and you dismiss it all like it's nothing! What am I supposed to do with this?! I just don't know what to think anymore, and it is SO HARD being in the middle ALL THE TIME!"

Shaking and with frantic eyes darting around the room, I must look like a cornered animal. I never speak to my parents without my guardrails: politeness, restraint, diplomacy, fear, shame, but the words leapt out of me. What a terrifying, electric, guts-on-the-table experience it is to say how you feel. I hate feeling this out of control, but I had no choice. When my reality is rejected with abandon, I can't stay quiet.

I know you love me, but do you believe me? It hurts to not be believed.

Mom and Dad look at me, agape.

"Oh, Susan, we don't mean to make you feel that way," she says softly.

"No," Dad says, perplexed. They look shocked.

Have I been hiding my feelings THAT well?

"It's just so hard," I reiterate quietly, my ears ringing. I replay my outburst in my head, combing over each word guiltily in case I overreacted or should apologize.

NO. I said my honest feelings that have been building for years, and I don't regret it. Today, their baseless ravings have consequences.

"We don't have to talk about anything that makes you upset," Dad says. Mom nods slowly and looks at me with a pained face.

While I appreciate their caring reaction, I hate feeling like I'm the problem here, like the issue is my ineptitude at coping with a complex world rather than their idiotic gullibility. Our inability to transcend never-ending conflicts and reach some higher plane of understanding and peace with each other has me utterly defeated.

In my worst thoughts, thoughts I am not proud of, I want a tragedy to happen close to them. I don't want them to be hurt, of course, but I want them to hear sirens, see police tape and chaos, follow breaking news, talk to first responders and victims, and get grounded for fuck's sake. Their lives are so insular that everything happens far away to people they don't know or care about, so it can all be carelessly dismissed.

I open Instagram on my phone and start scrolling while my body's still on fire.

I'll punish their nonsense with my silence.

Every other post pleads for the Mandalay Bay mass shooting to be the last. #PrayForVegas #guncontrol #thoughtsandprayers

After a few minutes, whatever she's reading on her laptop

makes Mom's eyes pop. "Susan, have you ever flown through the Denver airport?"

"Don't think so," I say, without looking up. Dad's re-arranging his pills.

"Well, good. There's all this strange art there apparently, and it was built on top of a bunker that's a safehouse for the Illuminati."

My eyes glaze over.

When will this ever end?

When I get home that night, Cary's on the phone with his parents and drinking a Pabst Blue Ribbon.

"She just walked in...Yeah, yeah...I'll tell her. Hey, Susan, my parents are coming to visit us for Christmas!" he says.

"Oh, great! Tell them they should stay with us!" I say.

They always generously host us when we visit their woodsy home in Washington. I take my rain gear off, then join Cary on a stool at our light wood bar, surrounded by our Ireland and Italy trip photos. In a green t-shirt, ragged jeans, and an old ballcap, he's the only person who feels like home to me.

"Yes, you should stay with us! We have the extra bedroom," he says into the phone.

"Ooo, we could take them to Solvang!" I whisper. The adorable Danish town a few hours north is our go-to with visitors and is especially festive around the holidays. He pitches the idea to his parents, then gives me a thumbs up.

"That is near Susan's parents, yeah," Cary says into the phone. "Well...sure, we could see them on the way...yeah, you can all finally meet! After nine years!" he laughs.

FUCK FUCK FUCK FUCK

My heart starts to pound.

When Cary gets off the phone, he notices my panic-stricken face.

"What's wrong?" he says, scratching his beard. He flips his cap backwards.

I've always expected our parents, all born-again Christians, to get along famously, and Cary's parents know about my parents' quirks. But it's been personally advantageous to keep them apart.

"If our parents are going to meet, and your parents are staying with us," I say, piecing everything together, "I should probably come clean and tell my parents that we live together."

FUCK FUCK FUCK FUCK

Cary's sibling has led such a reckless life that our unmarried cohabitation doesn't faze his parents, but I've never had a fuck-up brother or sister help lower my parents' expectations.

"I'm not going to ask your parents to lie for me. That'd be silly. But it might come up while they're all together, and it'd be embarrassing for my parents to find out that way."

FUCK FUCK FUCK FUCK

This is the moment I've been anxiously avoiding since The Great Virginity Loss of 2008: when my parents discover I'm no longer a Christian saving herself for marriage.

Maybe I should be grateful for the years of conspiracy theory diversion that have kept my parents' focus off my personal life.

"It's probably time they know anyway," I say, trying to convince myself. A 32-year-old woman in this day and age telling her parents she lives with her longtime partner shouldn't be a thing, but my pounding heart begs to differ.

Cary shrugs, finishes his beer, and heads to the fridge for another. He's eight years older than me. He gives fewer fucks.

I've been lying to protect you, too, ya know, Cary. When my parents finish casting Satan out of me, you'll be next.

I follow him to the fridge for a beer and try to formulate the words that will break my parents' hearts.

FUCK FUCK FUCK FUCK

CHAPTER 29
FLAT EARTH DAY

"AND YOU WILL KNOW the truth, and the truth will set you free."

    -John 8:32

~32~

I should get it over with right away, as soon as I walk in:

Happy Thanksgiving, Mom and Dad! Cary and I live together! Pass the stuffing!

Dressed like a cliché Southern Californian in Fall in a brown sweater, dark jeans, and boots, I chew my lip the whole drive to Santa Barbara to spend turkey day with my parents. It's the last day I'm going to see them before they meet Cary's parents on Christmas Eve, so it's now or never.

Dad called Mom 'Marie Andretti' in her speeding ticket days and always tells me, "You've got a lead foot just like your mother." Today, though, in no hurry to my Judgment Day, I'm driving up the 101 at the speed limit for once.

Everything changes today. Everything changes today.

I park in the last available and farthest guest spot at my

parents' community, then look into my pulsing blue eyes in the rearview mirror and promise myself I won't chicken out.

You HAVE to tell them. It's time. Be a big girl.

I walk across the long parking lot under the bright sun, unsure if I'm sweating from nerves or the temperature.

In the packed lobby, residents proudly show off the grand piano, the library, and the other community perks to their holiday visitors. I turn left down a long hallway, and as I approach my parents' door, I hear Mom laughing her head off.

At least she's in a good mood.

My knuckles tap our signature knock on their dark brown door.

"Ahahaha! Oh! Come on in!" she sings.

"Well, something must be funny," I say as I enter.

Preferably something that would perfectly segue into my announcement.

Lying in her tan velvet recliner, she's all gussied up in a gold shimmery turtleneck, black jeggings, and extra bright makeup for the holiday. She continues laughing with her mouth wide open while her eyes gleam from behind her long blonde bangs and clear, big glasses.

"Susan, have you seen these skits? They're a riot!"

I sit while she swivels her laptop toward me. It's a still of Melissa McCarthy playing Press Secretary Sean Spicer on *Saturday Night Live.*

"I have! That's Melissa McCarthy. She's hilarious. I'm surprised *you* find this funny," I say with a smirk.

Shouldn't you consider her blasphemous for making fun of your president's staff?

Mom continues playing the clip, and we laugh together as McCarthy/Spicer angrily yells at the press, sticks wads of gum under the podium, answers questions using ridiculous props, and then zips around on a Segway.

Dad slowly plods into the living room, his cane-assisted

walking looking arduous. He falls into his recliner and laughs along with us at the sketch.

Enjoy this rare moment of levity with your parents, Susan. It might be your last.

"I hope the drive up wasn't too bad," Mom says, putting away her laptop when we finish the clip. "How's L.A. these days?"

Oh, everyone's polyamorous now. Explaining that would make your head explode.

"I have good news! I've been cast in a new comedy at a really great theatre on the West Side. I'm the understudy for the female lead, but I have a few guaranteed performances."

"Oh, great!" Mom says.

"Congratulations!" says Dad. "When do you start practicing?"

After all these years, Dad, c'mon.

"I'm only going to have a few *rehearsals*," I correct him, "in December before opening night, so I'm doing a ton of memorizing now. Dad, remember those clips you showed me once of a man with a mustache ranting about the American government being bloated, incompetent, stifling individual liberty, etc.?"

"Oh, yeah!" Dad says, laughing all over again. Ron Swanson, played by Nick Offerman on *Parks and Recreation*, is a pop culture hero in Dad's online libertarian world.

"That actor has performed at this theatre and actually met his wife there, Megan Mullaly, when they did a play together. She's famous, too…" I continue rambling about them and their work, the time I saw Mullaly on Broadway, my audition for *Parks and Recreation*, my friends who've been on it…

C'mon, Susan! Get to it already!

Mom looks at her watch.

"It's just about time for our dining room reservation for lunch. Shall we?" she asks.

Well, so much for coming clean right away. How on the flat earth are they going to take this news?

Dad gets in his red scooter and buzzes ahead, a thin, gray-haired figure in a crisp white collared shirt hunched over his mini racecar. We make our way down several long, tasteful but older hallways to the community dining room, and I walk slower to stay by Mom's side, who waddles in an off-balanced way that makes her trajectory more zig-zag than straight.

We arrive at our reserved table for the annual Thanksgiving buffet that always includes a raw seafood spread, an omelet bar, the obligatory turkey, and an array of salads, dressings, sides, and desserts. Elderly residents in their Sunday best glow with joy to have family visiting them. Today and Christmas are the only days I see children here.

Should I break the news to them here? Will they be less inclined to make a scene? Safety in numbers?

Mom and I dodge scurrying kids and slow-moving older folks overwhelmed by all the buffet options as we fill our plates and make one for Dad, then we return to our table.

"Cary wishes he could be here, but he had to work today-" I start to say as I dive into my favorite part of the Thanksgiving meal: the stuffing.

"Oh, Susan, that's the couple we told you about, Steve and Debbie, with the son going through the divorce," Mom says, pointing with her fork to an older couple across the room.

"Oh?" I say, turning around to see.

"It's just terrible. Their son is a doctor, too!" Mom says.

"Well, Cary's parents are really looking forward to meeting you both next month. They usually host Christmas, so-"

"Chris!" Dad exclaims as a gaudily dressed, large woman passes us with a mound of food.

"Oh, John! Dawn! Hi!" the animated woman replies. Her enormous rings and bracelets jangle as she waves. "I sure hope you don't hear my heels stomping around! I'm always worried about that! Happy Thanksgiving, everybody!" she says before prancing off.

Dad leans over to me. "Chris lives above us and is always

worried about her heels bothering us. I always tell her we don't hear a thing!" he laughs.

It's hard to not get depressed coming here.

Is this my future: repetitive conversations, using a scooter, and waiting for the holidays when family will make the effort?

Hm, what family will I have?

Eventually, I give up trying to contribute and just nod and gasp when appropriate as my parents incessantly whisper to me about other residents.

When we get back to their apartment, Dad says, "Well, I need a nap after all that," then drives his scooter to his room.

Dangit. I can't tell just Mom by herself.

She falls into her recliner, and I sit in my usual chair.

"Susan, isn't it suspicious that the Queen of England is as healthy as she is at her age? I think it's because the elite must have access to special drugs or vitamin shots or serums or something. Princess Di and I have the same maiden name, you know. We're royalty, Susan…"

This one again.

I listen and nod, but all I can think about is getting MY BIG LIE off my chest as soon as Dad returns. An hour later, he does.

Here's your moment, Susan!

I reach into my bag, pull out a copy of *Santa Barbara Magazine* that I nabbed at a gas station just before arriving, and flip through it.

You're stalling, Susan!

I know! Shut up!

Articles about local restaurant openings, upcoming festivals, and wineries spark inspiration for breath-of-fresh-air experiences with my parents, only to be dashed by their imagined responses: "too many steps for Daddy," "too many people," "why would we go to a winery?" This suffocating wacko echo chamber of a living room is the only place they're comfortable.

The hours pass, and I can't muster the courage to confess my sin, despite my rising blood pressure and splitting stress headache. My fear of the unknown and of breaking the last thread of a bond that we have is too much. It's planted so deeply in me to never ever ever disappoint them, so revealing that I've fully abandoned their religion, the most precious part of their lives, may devastate all three of us.

Finally, by 9 pm, the latest I've ever stayed, I know I can't put it off any longer. It's time to head back to L.A., so it's time to spill. Mom and Dad are both reading in their recliners and have their reading lamps on full blast. The evening is painfully quiet.

Maybe this is better anyway. I'll say it, then run out the door.

I open my mouth, then close it.

I open my mouth again and almost make a sound, then stop.

JUST GET IT OVER WITH, SUSAN!

"Well, I should get going," I say, but my body stays seated while my heart races.

YOU CAN'T GET UP UNTIL IT'S OVER, SUSAN!

"Okay," Mom sighs. Dad nods. They look ready for me to leave.

"But there's something I should tell you before I go," I say finally, my voice shaking.

The energy in the room changes. Time slows. I feel them snap to DEFCON 1.

"What?" Dad shoots out quickly, more alert than I've seen him in a long time.

"Oh?" Mom says curiously, sitting up.

I'll play this scene as humbly as I can, dripping with shame for my wicked soul. I'll throw myself on the mercy of the court, mournful eyes pleading for grace. The more pathetic, the better. Who can kick a kitten?

"You should know that Cary and I actually-"

I can't believe I'm saying this!

"-live together."

Should I specify how long? For five deceitful, sinful years?

Absolutely not.

I hold my breath and wait for their response. Gears grind behind their poker faces.

Say something! Say something! Say something!

"Well, that's what I figured," Mom says gently.

Flabbergasted, my heart stops.

Are you serious? My approach worked! My pained demeanor must have activated her nurturing side. Or she's not as naïve as I pegged her.

Maybe somewhere deep down, underneath the extreme beliefs she espouses day in and day out, there's still a piece of her that's in touch with the sinful world she left behind, the one where unmarried adults sleep together, shack up, and hope for the best.

Relief, like a bucket of water dumped on my head, washes over me, and my headache fades. It's over.

"Now we would prefer you two be married and hope you consider that in the future," she adds slowly.

"I understand," I reply, shocked by such a normal parental statement from my anything-but-normal parents. "Thank you-"

For not saying I'll burn in hell?

"-for being so...nice...about it," I awkwardly mumble, breathing normally for the first time today. I grab my purse and stand up. "All right, see you at Christmas!"

"We'll see you then," Mom says with a tired smile.

Dad looks lost in thought.

I bounce out, 20 pounds lighter, and on the other side of the door, exhale deeply.

Wow, did I stress about this for years for no reason?

CHAPTER 30
FLAT EARTH RISING

(THIS IS where I'd quote a Bible verse that explicitly condemns pre-marital sex, but I couldn't find one.)

~32~

Three weeks later, I'm lying in bed in my fuzzy pink PJs and glasses, my face illuminated by my phone, when my doom-scrolling is interrupted by a late-night email from Dad. I click on it, and my eyebrows raise when I see how long it is.

"Dear Susan, you surprised me when you told your mom and me that you and Cary live together. It should come as no surprise that I think a man and woman living together is a mistake."

Here comes the condemnation I was expecting.

I was so relieved by Mom's surprisingly calm reaction that I mistook Dad's silence as agreement.

"Now God is a good God and does not desire harm to anyone. But He cannot bless a man and woman simply living together," Dad's email continues.

God's omnipotent powers stop there?

"I also perceive that you and Cary have certain differences.

You're a vegan, and he's a meat-eater. You come from different financial and intellectual/academic backgrounds. You are a go-getter, Cary is more laidback…"

Ah, ha! You think I can do better. Is that the real problem?

And I was only briefly vegan, like most of my Angelino brethren. Keep up, Dad.

He closes with the "men marry women hoping they don't change, but they do, and women marry men hoping to change them, but they don't" bit as a caution to avoid disappointment.

You're really selling it, Dad.

Reading his admonishment from the comfort of my condo, surrounded by all that Cary and I have built together: the furniture we found at thrift stores, our travel photos and movie posters on the walls, the swag everywhere that we get as theme park employees, the memories of hosting our friends here often, I don't feel any guilt for sharing my life, and my body, which is the real issue, with someone I love.

Why is the need to control sexuality embedded so deeply in Christianity?

I start typing my response: "Dad, thank you for sharing your thoughts with me. Respectfully, I disagree." Then I cite real-world examples of Christian couples we know who've bitterly divorced and my unreligious, unmarried friends in long, supportive relationships.

If my experiences refute what the Bible says, how can it be The Truth?

My bible is a collection of learned wisdom from a variety of sources, but mostly trial and error, missteps and wins, and a life spent observing humans:

Relationships 12:17: "Thou shouldst walk away before saying something thou will regretest."

Theatre 1:4: "She who prepareth gettith the part."

Jobs 9:13: "Don't shit where you eat."

Imperfect and always under review as it may be, I know the

why behind my commandments, and real-world experience backs each of them up.

More than anything, though, the reason I can't appease my parents by getting hitched is this: marriage still gives me the willies. I'm terrified of being trapped. What if I marry a sweet guy in my youth who turns into a flat earther in our 70s? CAN YOU IMAGINE? And don't get me started on the obscene cost, archaic traditions, and ludicrous wedding expectations that offend my extreme practicality. When my first bridesmaid's dress, a poop-colored handmaid number, cost $118, I thought *Allison, are you insane?*

Re-reading the email I thought would shatter me, I realize how unshakeable my convictions are now. The most meaningful part of my life is living with Cary, even if he does leave his used cups everywhere.

CHAPTER 31
MEET THE FLAT EARTHERS

"GOOD TIDINGS we bring to you and your kin,
   We wish you a Merry Christmas and a happy New Year!"
   -Unknown author

~32~

"Susan, these date bars are delicious. I'm so touched that you remembered they're my favorite," Cary's dad, George, bellows from the back seat in his booming voice. Scrunched into my Prius, wearing a simple white shirt and crinkly khakis, he looks like an amiable giant crammed into a toy car while he nibbles away.

"I can't believe how early you got up to make them before we headed out for Santa Barbara today," Cary's mom, Patty, says while looking out the window. The glare makes her pale, makeupless face even paler, and her short, straight red hair appear light orange.

Am I trying to solidify my good reputation with them before they meet my parents? Probably.

"Merry Christmas Eve!" I reply with a grin as I drive us up

the 101. Cary smiles at me from the passenger seat and pats my thigh. I go above and beyond for all parents, it seems.

"Now you've told us about your parents over the years-" George starts, and I feel myself tense up despite his warmth. "-and we thanked the Lord this morning for bringing us all together today and that we get to meet some fellow believers! Didn't we, Patty?" he says, looking over at her.

She nods, but her focus stays on the rugged cliffs and ocean scenery basking under the bright sun. This is not her typical December day in Washington.

"And I've told them about you, like how you were a chaplain on ride-alongs with the police, George. They were very impressed. I think you'll have a lot in common. Except for the conspiracy theories," I laugh.

Please find that funny.

"Right!" George guffaws and slaps his knee. I catch Patty's eyebrows furrow while she looks out the window.

Please don't hold their craziness against me, Patty.

Eventually, we pull into the bustling parking lot of my folks' retirement community, busy with young guests in holiday attire eager to see grandma and grandpa.

"So, this is where my parents live. That's the assisted living wing over there," I say, pointing to the smaller tan stucco building with a Spanish tile roof. "They have a memory care unit in there. But this," I say, gesturing to the longer building with a large wooden castle-like entrance, "is the independent living area where my parents have a little two-bedroom apartment. We can all have lunch together in the community dining room after you see their place, then we can head to Solvang for the rest of the day if that sounds good."

"Well, sure! Sounds great!" George booms.

"This is very nice," Patty says, with worried eyes. She looks insecure as she smooths down her plain blue shirt and pats down her hair.

"We're just along for the ride this whole trip. Take us

anywhere you want!" George adds with a smile, as laid-back a houseguest as you can ask for.

"Dad, don't miss the flat earth posters," Cary says into the rearview mirror with a wink.

"Oh, boy!" George says with a big laugh. Patty shakes her head.

I know, Patty, I know.

We all get out of the car, and I giggle to myself watching Cary and his mom, two stocky figures with thick middles and hunched shoulders, walk in the baby step shuffle that they do. George towers over the three of us.

Even though my mom could detour us into Crazytown at any moment, I trust that our parents, four born-again Christians, will have plenty of common ground to fill a lunch. Not being the sole conversation partner to my mom's shenanigans is, frankly, a welcome reprieve.

I lead us to my parents' apartment door and knock. "We're here! Anybody home?"

I hear footsteps on the other side.

"Hi! Come on in!" Mom says as she opens the door wide. Her blonde hair is extra teased, lipstick extra pink, and outfit extra Christmas: black pants, red turtleneck, and a busy red and gold jacket with thick shoulder pads. Just over her heart sits a shiny Christmas tree brooch that used to be Grandma's.

I introduce everyone as we walk in, and high-spirited overlapping chatter ensues. Dad walks into the living room with his cane, and he wears his usual business attire even though he's been retired for years. He falls into a chair and gives Cary the usual keep-your-distance handshake.

"Cary," Dad says with a closed-mouth smile.

"Good to see you, John," Cary says, unable to hide his laughter at the obvious awkwardness of them shaking hands after knowing each other for eight years now.

"I hope you had a nice drive up! Let me give you the tour!" Mom says. I smile watching her play the part of exuberant hostess with gusto. "We are so happy here. They've got every-thing! Here's the patio…"

As she walks us through the living room, I clock George registering the flat earth posters. He raises an eyebrow at Cary, who suppresses a smirk and nods.

Mom elaborates on the community's amenities, interesting residents, excellent medical care, and how safe they feel.

"So, have I sold you? Gonna move here?" she says with a big smile to button her pitch.

"We'll take it!" George exclaims, then he laughs heartily, which delights my mom to no end.

Patty looks overwhelmed. "Everything is so…nice," she sighs.

Once we're seated for lunch in the dining room, I relish getting to sit back for a change. Cary and I let the adults talk, and the conversation goes exactly where I knew it would: the state of the evangelical church today, cornerstone Bible verses, and each believer's life-changing come-to-Jesus moment. My eyes meet Cary's across from me at the large circular table. He gives me a discreet smile while his father solemnly shares how he became born-again.

"I met a man who took me into his home and told me about Jesus. He basically became my father."

"Oh my," my mom says, caught up in his story. She covers her mouth with her hand.

"I even took his last name," George continues. "I was so lost in my youth. The '60s. Whew!" he exclaims, shaking his head at the dark period in his life before finding Christianity.

Then his face brightens. "But I was never lost enough to get into drugs, praise the Lord!" he laughs.

"Well-" Mom says, then she stops herself and looks at my dad with a know-it-all expression.

Brace yourselves, everybody!

"Well, I don't know if you'll receive this, but our government introduced LSD onto college campuses in the '60s to subdue all the anti-war student protests. It just knocked them all out, so we could stay in Vietnam," she says, matter-of-factly.

George and Patty politely nod, and I observe their wheels turning on how to respond.

It's hard, right? Although, honestly, this one's more plausible than her others.

"How did they introduce it?" Patty asks, confused.

The question route. That's my go-to. Solid choice, Patty.

"Oh, they had undercover agents disguised as students who passed it out at parties and got everyone addicted." Mom looks more like she's theorizing on the spot as opposed to repeating something she read. Everyone ponders this until George breaks the silence.

"Well, they should have been handing out haircuts! As lost as I was, I was never a long-haired hippie, praise the Lord!"

Everyone chuckles, and the conversation relaxes back into uncontroversial territory until lunch concludes and we bid my parents goodbye.

"We almost got out of there without a conspiracy theory!" Cary laughs when we get back in my car with his parents.

"Dawn needs to get back in the Word," Patty says with pursed lips as she folds her arms and looks out the window. George nods.

"Yup," I say.

Sure, that's it.

I turn the car on and start backing up. "To Solvang?"

"To Solvang!" George and Patty say in unison.

As our light-hearted day in the adorable Danish town unfolds, I feel a new sense of wholeness. The worlds I've kept separate out of paralyzing fear: the Santa Barbara parents mind-fuck and my personal life with Cary, have entwined like never before, and everyone survived. That night, with one week until the new year, I fall asleep blissfully anticipating how much more honest and connected next year will be.

CHAPTER 32
SALT OF THE
FLAT EARTH

"FLAT EARTHERS ARE the biggest victims of their beliefs."
   -Kelly Weill

~33~

When my phone vibrates on the vanity in my dressing room, I put down my mascara and see that it's Dad calling.

He only calls when it's serious.

Too nervous to answer, I let it ring and finish applying mascara and curling my hair for my theme park shows that day. It's May 1, and the last time I saw my parents was Christmas Eve when they met Cary's parents.

Mom has canceled every planned monthly visit since, citing some degree of "not feeling well." She won't see a doctor since she has dismissed them all as scam artists complicit with greedy pharma, so her latest self-diagnosis is fatty liver disease. According to her research, it can be reversed with a diet change, so she's been focusing on that to cure her mystery illness.

When she canceled last month, I pushed harder, saying that I wanted to be helpful if she was sick and the visit could be brief if she was tired. She declined.

My phone buzzes with a voicemail notification, and I stare at it with foreboding curiosity.

I do have 10 minutes before my show starts.

I grab my phone, exit the dressing room, and go into the gray, industrial stairwell in our theatre for privacy. I hit 'Play' on the voicemail and press the phone close to my ear so I can hear it over the roller coaster screams and blaring atmosphere music.

"Hi, Susan, it's Dad. Give me a call back when you can. Bye," he says in his usual over-the-phone stilted cadence. Since he sounds normal, I call back. My eyes stare at the ground while it rings.

"Hi, Susan," he answers flatly.

"Hey, Dad, I have a few minutes before my show. What's up?"

"Well, your mother fell the other day. She couldn't get up, so they took her to the hospital and found that she has cancer," he says, slowly but matter-of-factly.

Breathe.

"It's too far along to do chemo or anything-"

Breathe.

"-not that she would anyway." I picture him shaking his head, bewildered at her conspiracy theory-induced mistrust of doctors and treatments. "So, she's just resting at home. We'll have caregivers here around the clock, and a doctor's coming over tomorrow. We'll see what he says we can do."

What am I supposed to say, what am I supposed to say...

"Okay, Dad. Thank you for telling me. However I can help, let me know. My next day off is Thursday. I can come up then if that's okay?"

"That's fine. We'll see you then." Click.

Instantly, I'm the numb, helpless 10-year-old I was when Daddy had a stroke.

What am I supposed to do, what am I supposed to do...

"Places," our stage manager's voice says through the intercom.

The only way to get through my four shows today is to forget this call ever happened, so I wipe my memory clean, march back into the dressing room, drop my phone on the vanity, and head downstairs to the stage with a smile. I catch myself in the last mirror, taking in my corporate host look: wedge heels, tan nylons, tight gray skirt, and purple plaid collared shirt.

Look at that show makeup and hair! I look great! Everything's going to be fine! Let's have fun today!

Compartmentalizing is key to performing day in and day out.

At the bottom of the stairs, I take a sharp left, then right, and cross through the dark backstage. While the pre-show music swells, I walk onto the stage where a giant movie screen and a few feet in front of that, a giant black curtain, stand between me and a small buzzing morning audience in our 1,700-seat theatre.

Cancer, cancer, ca-

No! Kittens and flowers! Kittens and flowers!

I walk around the screen and into the small space just behind the center of the curtain, where a crew member, Herbert, awaits me. He will cue me to step through the curtain and onto the stage when the stage manager says in his headset, "Host A Go."

"Hey!" he says to me with a mischievous grin, in his crew blacks. "Okay, your word is 'spaghetti.' You have to work 'spaghetti' into the show somewhere," he giggles. This is our game whenever he's working.

Too far along to do chemo, too far along to do-

"Spaghetti, spaghetti, spaghetti," I repeat, thinking through where I can work that word into our show about how movies are made.

The trick knife stage blood part! Something about the blood looking like spaghetti sauce! Boom!

"I got it! Don't miss it this time," I say, playfully swatting his arm. "I'm always so proud of myself when I work your word in, and then you don't hear it!" I laugh.

He smiles and shrugs. Then I hear the footsteps of my energetic co-host, Erik, approach from the other side of the movie screen until his gray shadow is just on the other side of me.

"Susan, you there?" he shouts.

I'm trying to be.

"Heck yeah! Let's do this!" I say.

We both raise our hands to the screen, and after a beat, we holler in unison, "It's the first show of the daaaaaaaaaay!" while we slap each other's hands over and over with the screen between us like it's a giant bongo drum. This is our sacred routine before every show together.

The pre-show music ends, the lights fade to black, and in the silence, I watch Herbert. He concentrates on hearing the cue in his headset.

My mother is dying.

"Aaaaaand go!" he whispers while he pages the curtain for me.

My mother is dying.

With a confident smile and over-the-top show energy, I make my entrance.

My mother is dying.

CHAPTER 33

MY EARTH GOES FLAT

"JESUS WEPT."
  -John 11:35

~33~

I wait to tell Cary about Mom's diagnosis until we're both home from work that night. He goes pale and quiet, my reaction reflected back to me.

I do another day at work just like the last, performing two different shows: the one onstage where I'm an upbeat, unflappable host and the one offstage where I'm a carefree co-worker during green room chitchat. I think I'm supposed to be hysterical or inconsolable, but I feel nothing, numb, empty.

Should I be dropping everything? No one's telling me to rush home.

On Thursday, I take in the coastal scenery all the way to my parents' place in deafening silence. No music. No podcasts. Just my muted thoughts.

How many times have I done this drive? How many more times will I do it?

I park and approach their building, unsure of what to expect, trying to be ready for anything. Goosebumps cover my exposed arms, the downside of wearing a pink T-shirt Mom gave me on a cool, spring morning. Over my shoulder is a colorful gift bag for Mom's birthday, the one I had ready for last month's canceled visit, and as I walk down the hallway toward their door, its contents clink and clank together.

My eyes dart for clues once their door is in sight. It's ajar. *That's unusual.*

I open it slowly and peek my head in. With the blinds to the patio closed and only one lamp on, it's strangely dark. The flat earth posters are just gray blurs in the dim lighting. Dad sits at the small breakfast table with his back to me, hunched over medical brochures and pills. Across from him, in my usual seat, is a tired nurse in her 40s.

"You must be Susan," she says as I slowly walk in.

"Yeah," I say softly.

"I'm Courtney, your mom's hospice nurse."

Dad twists around as best he can to see me. His eyes are sunken in, and his shoulders slumped, his short hair all gray. I sit in Mom's tan recliner. It's odd to view this familiar room, one that's usually so brightly lit, from a new spot. More of the tiny kitchen is visible from here, with its mini fridge, a few appliances, and bare walls.

Someone tell me what to do, the anxious 10-year-old inside me begs.

"Hi, Susan. She's resting, but you can go in her room and see her," Dad says, encouragingly.

"No, that's okay," I say, putting my purse and the gift bag down beside the recliner. "I won't bother her if she's trying to sleep."

"I'm sure she'd love to see you," the nurse says.

"That's okay." My body rigidly commits to staying seated.

Seeing her will make it all real, just like when I saw Dad in the hospital after his stroke. That's when everything changed.

"How is she?" I ask.

"Tired," he says. "Sleeping a lot."

"The meds we've got her on are just to make her comfortable so she's not in pain. I don't know what you know, but it's stage four," she says gently. "Breast cancer. The doctor yesterday estimated she may have a couple of months."

I should be here more.

Immediately, my brain calculates a new schedule: I can arrange to work every other day to keep my usual four days of theme park shows per week and drive up to Santa Barbara every other day in between.

The nurse goes to check on her, leaving Dad and me alone: two under-reactive, reserved people used to letting Mom lead the conversation.

"What happened?" I ask after a minute.

I mean that on so many levels.

He sighs. "She hasn't had much energy for months. I told her to see a doctor, but she never wanted to go or even felt up to going. I insisted and finally found one who makes house calls, but she didn't like the way he poked and prodded her. That ended quickly," he says, rolling his eyes and laughing to himself. Then the humor drains from his face.

"When she fell trying to get out of bed and couldn't get back up on Monday, the paramedics had to come to lift her. They were worried she had a broken bone or something, so they took her to the hospital. The scans showed cancer. Everywhere." He hangs his head, and his eyes search the ground.

I nod along, waiting for these life-changing words to prick my eyes with emotion, but I just sit there.

Maybe I'm in shock?

Dad fidgets with the splint that holds his paralyzed left arm, and I sit there wondering what to do next.

"She doesn't know you're here, you know," he says after a few minutes. "You can go in."

"No, if she's resting, I'll wait till she's awake."

"You should see her," Dad says finally, pointedly.

I take a deep breath.

The moment of truth.

"Okay." I grab Mom's birthday gift bag, head to the hall, and with my back touching the wall opposite her bedroom door, I peer in.

One bedside lamp illuminates the small, undecorated room and makes the white walls appear honey-colored. The nurse is bent over the bed, talking to her softly.

"Oh, Dawn, look! Your daughter's here!" the nurse says brightly when she turns around and sees me.

I force a smile and wave awkwardly. My degree might be in drama, but I'm total chicken shit when it comes to the real thing.

Mom looks right at me with a confused face, the exact way Grandma looked at me from her deathbed, and an eerie, unsettling, familiar feeling flutters in my stomach. Mom squints through her big, clear glasses, then puts it all together.

"Oh, Susan," she says weakly with heavy lips.

"Hi, Mom."

Her short hair is thin and frizzy, the blonde so pale it looks almost white, as does the rest of her makeupless face above her white nightgown and white sheets.

"All right, I'll be here if you need anything," the nurse says to Mom before exiting.

I walk into her bedroom, which contains a twin bed in the center, a large white dresser in the corner, a tray that can be wheeled over the bed, a bedside commode, and a folding chair next to her head. I sit in it and instinctively lean in close because she clearly doesn't have the energy to sit up or see very well. Even though we are not a touchy family, without thinking, I clutch her heavy hand.

What am I supposed to say?

"It's good to see you after so long, Mom. How are you?"

"Well, how about this?" she says, twisting her mouth into a side smirk that Grandma used to do. "Cancer. Huh." She shakes her head slowly as if to acknowledge that her self-diagnosis of fatty liver disease was all wrong.

I pull out her birthday gifts one by one, all kitschy items from her favorite road trip spot that just opened a California location: Cracker Barrel. She follows the items with her eyes since she can barely move her head, and she smiles weakly at each.

"Your birthday gifts are over there," she says, pointing with her eyes toward the top of her dresser at a few plastic bags of clothes. "Had them since February. Gosh." She shakes her head again, slowly. "I meant to wrap them, but…" She loses steam and looks out of breath.

I fill the silence by telling her about the Kauai trip I just took with my friend Lisa.

"Is she still seeing the Egyptian?" Mom whispers. Dawn loves relationship gossip best.

"Yes," I lie. The complex cultural issues they broke up over are too much to explain at a time like this.

She starts blinking and murmuring about her eyes as she slowly reaches for the eye drops by her bedside and twists off the cap. I watch as her weak arms can barely hold the tiny bottle in the air over her eyes and squeeze the drops. After a few agonizing minutes watching her struggle, I can't stand it anymore.

"Mom, let me help." I hold the bottle over her face and squeeze while she tries to hold her eyes open to receive the drops. Seeing her so feeble and helpless crushes me. She nods when she's done, and her sagging face looks exhausted.

"I'll let you rest, okay, Mom? But I'll be here all day."

Her eyelids close, and the corners of her mouth fall as she swiftly drifts to sleep. I turn her lights off as I exit.

She sleeps through the rest of my visit. And the one a few days later on Saturday, too. Focusing on my plan of visiting every other day gives me a comforting sense of control and short-sightedness. I haven't cried or told anyone besides Cary.

———

On Monday, my next visit, I'm Santa Barbara-bound on the freeway later in the morning than I'd planned, still recovering from last night's party for Cary and me celebrating 10 years together. Our oldest friends joined us at the bar we had our first date at, and until closing time, we drank to a decade spent forging a life together and pursuing dreams alongside our grab bag of nuts and strays.

Mom's probably sleeping anyway. She won't notice if I'm late.

Traffic slows as I barrel down the steep, windy Conejo Grade toward Camarillo, so I lean on the brakes. This sharp downhill bend flanked by rolling green hills demarcates leaving L.A.'s urban concrete sprawl and entering the outskirts, where farmland and newer communities enjoy wide streets and large homes.

Last night's love fest brings a smile to my face, still sporting last night's mascara. I didn't dare ruin the mood by bringing up Mom's diagnosis.

The fertilizer smell of produce fields in Oxnard wafts in when my phone rings. I get that queasy feeling again when I see it's Dad calling.

He's probably just checking in about my arrival time.

I hit the steering wheel button that answers the call through my car. Traffic slows more, creating a sea of condensing red lights ahead.

"Hello?"

"Susan?"

"Yeah, Dad?"

"Your mom just passed." He starts to sob.

Traffic stops. I hit the brakes and burst into tears.

CHAPTER 34
FLATLINING ON THE EARTH

"LIFE'S BUT A WALKING SHADOW, a poor player
    That struts and frets his hour upon the stage
    And then is heard no more. It is a tale
    Told by an idiot, full of sound and fury
    Signifying nothing."
    -*Macbeth*, Act 5, Scene 5, William Skaespeare

~33~

Dawn is dead.

The source of my life and my longest-running, deepest-held frustrations has left this whatever-the-fuck-shape Earth.

"Oh…no…really?" I muster to Dad on the phone while I sit in stopped traffic on the 101.

He regains his composure. "I suggest you pull off at the next exit. Take some time and get back on the road whenever you're ready," he says slowly.

Sniffling and shaking, I follow his directions and park near a barren, abandoned field. Once I turn the car off, tears roar out of my eyes, and my body convulses. I put my wet face in my hands. Regrets the size of Mount Everest create a tidal wave of agony I've never experienced before.

But I was on my way! If I had left earlier, I would have been there! I thought we were supposed to have months! I should have spent every day with her since Dad's call! I should have left work immediately! I should have forced a visit the last four months, even though she said she wasn't up to it! We should have made her see a doctor sooner! She might be alive if we had! Why was I gallivanting around Kauai when my 76-year-old mother was so obviously seriously ill? Why was I partying last night at a bar when it was my mom's last night alive? If I had known we had six days left, I would have spent every second with her!

With streaks of wet mascara on my cheeks, I call Cary at work and blubber through telling him the news. His calming voice soothes me, like stirring cream into bitter black coffee.

When the wave of grief, the first of many, I'm sure, seems to dissipate, I get back on the freeway. My mind races while the traffic inches along all the way to my parents' place.

No. My dad's place.

Realizing this monumental change triggers the second wave, but I force myself to drive safely even though tears blur my vision and my eyes long to close.

With a swollen face covered in snot and tear streaks, I park and stumble from my car to my *dad's* apartment.

Sob.

I beeline through the open door to his bedroom, where he sits at his desk like it's any other day, a small figure in crisp business attire swallowed by an enormous, cushy, rolling black office chair. When he turns around, though, his face is red, scrunched, and wet like mine. We hug and cry together, unselfconscious about our uncontrollable, gushing emotions. No one prepares you for days like this.

"Her breathing was difficult this morning," Dad says after we end our embrace. "Just after 11, she let out a gasp, kind of like a cry. Danielle, the caregiver, and I went in to check on her, and that was it. She was gone. Danielle closed her eyes." He hangs his head while trying to control his shallow breathing.

I nod along, imagining it, and can't forgive myself for not being there.

No second takes. No re-dos. No try-again-next-times.

"They're on their way now, the folks who remove the body. You can go in there and be with her until they get here," he says, nodding toward her room. My parents had everything set up years ago: caskets, the Bible verse for the headstone (1 Corinthians 15), and plots with ocean views picked out and paid for. The Huckles are nothing if not prepared.

I exit his room, walk down the hallway, look into Mom's room on the right, and see my first dead body: matted white blonde hair, closed eyes, pale, slightly sunken in cheeks, a nose that is already succumbing to gravity, taut mouth open, all else is covered by a tightly-pulled white sheet. The unnerving sight of a rigid, physical shell I know so well, but without the animation of breath and ideas, is beyond my comprehension. I feel like an animal with an instinctual brain who can't understand the life-less remains of one of its own, like a fox softly pawing another's cold, stiff body in confusion, head-cocked, eyes moist, and ears alert.

Is this overwhelmingly unsettling feeling why people make up stories about an afterlife?

I should count myself lucky that it's taken until age 33 to come face to face with death, given that my grandparents all died far away and without ceremony, but right now, I feel anything but.

I sit in the bedside folding chair and tears drip from my jaw.

Am I supposed to say goodbye as if she's here? How does one pay their respects?

Is her ghost here? Is her soul living on somewhere else? Do I believe any of that?

The answer hits me like a blaring alarm going off in my skull, and it is unequivocal:

NO! The god who permeated my being with fear, judgment, and self-doubt is not and never was. Anyone claiming to know for certain what lies beyond our physical world is either a lunatic or selling something. The religion that gave Mom's life meaning and purpose and propelled her into the idiotic dark crevasses of the internet was all a LIE and a colossal waste of energy.

Then, like a knife to the chest, I'm convicted of my cold judgment when I'm flooded with memories of her tremendous love for me and total devotion to my father, even in the face of his paralyzing stroke so long ago.

Mom spent her life caring for Dad and me! She showed her love in countless ways: questions, support, service, cards, gifts, handmade clothes and art, emails... She lit up a room with her exuberance. She was always just doing the best she could.

With my chest bursting from emotion, I realize the best thing for me to do is mentally say goodbye and thank her for all the good. I sit and stare at her for what feels like hours, trying to make sense of her life and life in general.

Eventually, two young men in cheap blue suits arrive with the appropriate somber, respectful mood while making quick work of what is obviously routine for them: removing dead bodies.

After they leave, I notice Dad is working on a long to-do list at his desk: notify hospice, notify friends/family, write obituary, call bank, funeral...

I would very much like to be busy, too.

"Dad, I can take care of her stuff if that would be helpful," I offer gently, knowing that's the sort of physical work that would be difficult for him. "I assume we want to donate most everything?"

"Yes, thank you," he says, relieved. "And, obviously, take whatever you want," he adds before turning back to his desk and hunching over his list.

I recall friends' appalling stories about family squabbles over who gets what after a death. But Dad and I are all who survive her, and we're both unsentimental about stuff. Operating with only the essentials is all my overdrive brain can handle. Something about emptying Mom's room and sending her things on a new journey invigorates me.

Why am I so anxious to move on?

I open the Pandora app on my phone and select the Hawaiian station. While soft ukulele music plays, I efficiently sort through her items one by one, putting my organizational skills to use. *I'm GREAT at this!* I think, blessedly distracted. When an item stirs a faint pang, I quickly shove it in the appropriate donation bag and focus on the next.

The small, pretty items on the top of her dresser, the ones that have always lived there no matter what home we were in, are all I set aside for myself: her rings, a wispy blue and purple scarf with butterflies, a mother daughter heart necklace I gave her as a teen, and a small, clear stained-glass case from a bygone era with a red rose design on the top.

My obsessive thoroughness propels me to examine the living room for Mom-only items that can go. I head straight for the flat earth books on the bookcase near the sliding door to the patio.

At least now Dad and I can be rid of these once and for all.

As I'm pulling them out, Dad hobbles in. We are both dry-eyed and task-focused now.

"Just confirming you don't want to keep these, Dad?" I say, holding up the three large books that I can't wait to expunge from this place and my life. My ego can't handle being associated with such lunacy. I'm practically salivating at the thought of adding these to the donation bags. Or better yet, the trash.

"What are they?" he says, squinting, while he leans on his cane.

"The flat earth books," I say with an attitude that even today's events can't water down.

"Oh, let's keep those. I'd like to go through them," he says, excitedly. "Put them out on the table, so I can get to them easily."

He exits the room with a surge of energy, as if now that she's gone and he really has time on his hands, he can get to the bottom of this once and for all.

My mouth hangs open. With my hand still holding the books in the air, I sit there dumbstruck.

I really thought he was humoring her to keep the peace.

My eyes land on the flat earth posters that my fingers are itching to rip down.

Guess those are staying, too.

My eyes glaze over.

How dangerously influential one's partner can be.

By early evening, I'm physically and emotionally drained when I get to the last room that could use my organizing services: the kitchen. My droopy eyes take in the unopened packages on the counter, the crusty dishes filling the sink, the bags of supplies that haven't been put away, and a haphazard stack of medical documents, folders, and pamphlets. Every surface has dust or grime signaling four months of a compromised couple's neglect.

Seated at the breakfast table where he's taking his evening pills, Dad notices my overwhelmed face.

"You should go home and rest."

It pains me to leave a task unfinished, but I know he's right.

"Okay, but I'll call in sick tomorrow and resume here."

I should call in sick for the rest of the week. I can't imagine summoning the energy it takes to be onstage.

I drive home in the dark in a daze. In silence, I pass familiar exits, curves in the road, and long stretches by the black, lapping ocean. Mother/daughter scenes from my past, in no particular order, click before me like I'm looking through a viewfinder. I'm numb as I watch one after another until I notice a gut-wrenching pattern. In every scene, I am hiding something from her.

I've spent so much of my life pretending, playing all sorts of characters: a devoted Christian, a perfect daughter, a good girlfriend, a confident actress. Then there are the characters I've played onstage. But what if pretending was only for the stage?

The pain that so much of my relationship with my loving but misguided mother was based on a fabricated version of myself triggers another swell of tears as a new, devastating awareness of death's finality permeates my cells.

You can never go back. It's over.

The black sky is thick with billowy gray clouds, only visible on this moonless night when I pass the city lights of Summerland, Carpinteria, Ventura…

Onstage, we strive for truth, but to be truthful offstage? In real life? The stakes were always too high! Prioritizing everyone else's comfort seemed like the right thing to do. Following the rules and never questioning them was the safe way to blend in. Meeting others' expectations kept life blissfully simple.

…Oxnard, Camarillo, Thousand Oaks, the cities that make up L.A.'s sprawl grow denser, practically indecipherable from each other. I take my exit, Cahuenga Blvd., and slow to a stop at the red light at the end of the exit ramp. That's when a new awareness of my personal responsibility sets in, the kind that creeps up in the absence of a dominating authority figure.

It was my choice all along. I chose the roles and how I played them. I feared the consequences of being myself, of not being good enough, of being rejected, of being rebuked. I don't know how I'm going to flip the script, but I have to. Life is so achingly brief. This is the one time I'm here. Why spend one second being false?

CHAPTER 35
THE FLAT EARTH
KEEPS...SPINNING?

"ALWAYS GIVE yourself fully to the work of the Lord, because you know that your labor in the Lord is not in vain."
    -1 Corinthians 15:58

~33~

I drift through the ensuing days, fulfilling obligations but lethargic, weighed down by a profound sense of loss and re-examination.

I break down over planning Mom's funeral while having lunch at a restaurant with Cary.

"I don't know how to do this. I don't know how to do any of this," I sob in his arms in broad daylight. When the server cautiously checks in, I joke that I'm crying because the salad is that good.

Grief, even when it's in the background, eats up more energy than I could have imagined. I barely get through my theme park shows, so I drop out of a staged reading of a new musical. When my commercial agent drops me after not having booked a commercial in years, I'm relieved. I write to my longtime manager that I'm stepping back. I lean into the stability of my regular gig and the comfort of my chosen family there. I hold tightly onto Cary.

I now see my life in two pieces: before Mom died and after. My first lightbulb realization to guide my second act is that nothing's more important than how I spend my time. Grasping how abruptly it can be over, I now crave absolute satisfaction and meaning in whatever I'm doing, or it's out. I shake my head thinking about the hours I spent on shows that amounted to nothing, or the stress of running to casting offices all over town all year, to maybe spend one or two days on set. The ambition that dominated my identity evaporates into thin air.

With Mom gone, do I have no one to prove anything to anymore?

Or do I just not have the emotional energy to play pretend right now?

Her death confirms and compounds my other grief, the unspoken bleak hollowness that started creeping in as I drifted from Christianity, the sadness at seeing the world for what it is: utter chaos, terrifyingly unpredictable, tragically senseless. The true meaning of Christmas is merely a glimmer in the rearview now.

I long for deep meaning and a cosmic plan, but is that only because I was taught a grand, happy story early on? Which came first: the chicken with the savior and eternal life bit or the egg's existential need for a savior and eternal life?

———

I visit Dad every few weeks and take holidays off from my theme park show for the first time, so he doesn't spend them alone. Navigating our new one-on-one relationship means we catch up briefly, then spend afternoons reading separately and going on quiet drives, like to Dad's favorite beach in Goleta, the one we never went to because Mom didn't like it.

"This'll sound weird, Dad, but because of your stroke and all, did you think you would go first? I guess that's what I expected," I say carefully as we sit in the car in the Goleta Beach parking lot and stare at the water. An amateur surfer tests out the small waves in front of us.

"I did," he says, his dark blue eyes, the same color as the ocean, transfixed in the distance.

How can I tell him I love him and want to be there for him?

"Dad, I want you to know that you can talk to me about how you're really doing, if you're missing Mom or having a hard time."

"I'm just grateful for the time we had together," he says stoically, repeating his stock line these days.

To counteract the regret I have over hiding myself from Mom, I make a distinct effort to be more truthful with him, fearing the consequences less. When our conversation in the car leads me to mention a good friend of mine who happens to be gay, I seize the opportunity to state why I don't believe my dear friend's sexuality is wrong.

"But they have sex in their butts, Susan! And get diseases!" he says, horrified.

"Straight people do anal, too, Dad," I say calmly. "And get STDs."

He changes the subject, but I count the exchange as progress.

I also notice progress in how my hugs are received. I always sensed he preferred not to be touched, so I stayed away. Since Mom died, though, I've forced hello and goodbye hugs on him to utilize every tool at my disposal to make him feel loved. At first, he was noticeably thrown off and stiff, but now my heart melts a little when he reaches for me first.

When Dad transforms into a social butterfly, attending community events and reaching out to other residents to schedule meals together in the dining room, I'm delighted. When he becomes smitten with a new resident at his community, an attractive, petite blonde wearing Ann Taylor Loft, I'm happy for him. When I notice a few wall decorations are gone a few visits after meeting her, I'm thrilled!

"Dad, did you take down the flat earth posters?" I ask him casually, trying to hide my glee.

Sitting across from me at the small table in the living room, his eyes are buried in a book. "Yeah."

"How come?"

"They just don't need to be up anymore," he says without looking up.

I guess "Hey, did you know the Earth is flat?" didn't fly during date night chit chat. If he wanted another flat earther, there could be a dating app for that:

EDGE: We go to the very edge of the flat earth to find your soulmate!

In the basement of an undisclosed location that no surveillance gear can penetrate, EDGE matches meet in a bar-like ambiance surrounded by salt-of-the-Earth folks in American flag and "I Know Who Shot JFK" shirts.

"John," Dad's date from the app would say, with breathy delight, while she swirls her homemade moonshine in a jar and her handmade feather earrings dangle, "I looooove that you have your flat earth posters up loud and proud! Get over here, you free-thinking, populist, libertarian, you!"

They smooch, and then she invites him to her farmer's market booth, where she sells crystals, or her bootcamp for the zombie apocalypse, or her chemtrails protest. The Bible was right about one thing: a merry heart doeth good like a medicine.

———

With the help of therapy, I finally arrive at the conclusion that as long as I look at Mom's life through the lens of my standards and convictions, I'll be resentful and depressed. My bubbly, Millennial shrink, Cindy, urges me to take solace in the fact that Mom lived the life she wanted to, according to the beliefs that meant everything to her.

Just because I need physical evidence to believe, a product of lingering modernism perhaps, doesn't mean she did. Admittedly, though, I exercise faith in experts outside my field, like scientists and journalists, knowing they are fallible because I can't be everywhere and know everything. When I realize how frightening and malevolent the world must have seemed to her without trust in these institutions, empathy starts to bring me blessed peace.

Mom had a gullibility so innocent it was touching, but I can't blame her for being human and wanting hope. In an unstructured, atheistic existence, I continue to rediscover where my joy comes from: nurturing relationships, rapturous nature, art, and laughter. I hone in on what purpose means to me: being kind, generous, courageous, and loving. These are rewards unto themselves, however fleeting or happenstance. Maybe I have a fortitude Mom lacked that allows me to stare a godless existence in the face, or maybe life has just been kind enough to me that all is palatable sans deity so far.

Deep down, though, a biting fear nags:

How much have I evolved into my truest self, and how much have I absorbed the groupthink of my L.A. community, just as Mom was brainwashed by her online echo chamber?

This is the record's groove my needle always gets stuck in: discerning The Truth within the murky unknowable.

I don't miss navigating Mom's alternate reality and rigid religion, but I will spend the rest of my life unpacking her influence. More and more, I understand her melancholy, share her annoyances and mannerisms, and am rejuvenated by the same touchstones: my partner, the ocean, scenic drives, and stimulating reading, just with fewer conspiracy theories, I hope.

Now that I'm the age Mom was when she encountered the gospel, after losing her dad the same age I lost her, I see my parallel: a developing, consuming, lifestyle-changing tangent into sustainability and environmentalism. I'm no more immune to a cause that seems worthy and true than she was.

Somewhere in the recesses, though, the pain lingers from our lack of resolution and my inability to ever go back and do it all over again. The ache lies behind every smile and ordinary day and bubbles to the surface in quiet, private moments. It also fuels my determination to live honestly, to seek with courageous curiosity what deeper connection and understanding can be created when the layers of fear, dogma, and ego are stripped away.

I'm ashamed to say I underestimated the hole I'd be left with after her passing, the absence of her foundational, constant, familiar, and inflammatory presence that, in itself, is a comfort. Then there's the singular way I knew she loved me more than anyone else ever could or would.

ACT III

Three Years Later

CHAPTER 36

THE SUN SETS ON THE FLAT EARTH (SOMEHOW)

"WHATEVER PAIN you can't get rid of, make it your creative offering."

-Susan Cain

~36~

Dad and I sit quietly in his hospital room while Fox News plays muted on the TV. Seated at the foot of his bed, I see his eyes flash over something on the flat screen behind me.

"I don't know why the Democrats have it out for Trump!" he says, confused. His eyes bug out of his sun-spotted face while his white hospital gown and short, receding gray hair are askew. "What's not to like?"

A million reasons race through my head while his face relaxes into a knowing smirk and his eyes gleam. "Q says Trump will be restored to the presidency."

I close my eyes, and behind my mask, my mouth drops open. *Suspicions confirmed. Dad's gone full Q-Anon.*

"What about all the predictions by Q that have been wrong?" I ask, recalling Q's prophecy that Trump would be re-throned on

Biden's inauguration day earlier this year while an army of police hauled off the swamp in handcuffs.

"Some are wrong on purpose," Dad says with a twinkle in his eye.

My eyebrows raise.

"It throws off the other side," he adds with a grin.

I'm gobsmacked.

If what you believe can be flat-out wrong sometimes and you've found a way to justify that, too, then I give up. Fundamentalist Christians just can't resist a good story.

With his one working hand, Dad pats his favorite book about healing, *God Wants You Well*, that rests on his lap.

"I know you don't believe it, but Jesus is going to heal me," he says confidently. "I know it."

"That'd be great, Dad," I say honestly, with a shrug.

For all the times he's talked about healing, this is the first from his deathbed. At this point, though, challenging him would be cruel. After a month in this brand-new hospital in downtown Santa Barbara for late-stage kidney failure and daily flip-flopping between choosing dialysis or death, Dad has made his choice: neither, apparently.

Still crippled by overwhelming regret about how little I saw Mom at her end three years ago, I've dropped everything, seen him almost every day, and taken charge of his finances and medical care. Being an only child is one big party until it isn't.

The COVID-19 pandemic only shoved another wedge between us. When his community opened up after months on lockdown, and I visited wearing a mask, he scoffed. When I got vaccinated and asked if he was planning to, he snarled, "Over my dead body." The most excited I've seen him lately was when he received his ballot for a recall of our Democrat governor, someone he's furious with for mask mandates and interfering with businesses.

Dad's doctor, a diminutive blonde with a forlorn face, knocks and enters his spacious room decorated in shades of blue and cream.

"Hi, John, how are you doing today?"

"Well, I'd like to stop dialysis. I'm done with that," he says with a smile, as if they won't fight him as long as he's nice about it.

"Hm. What don't you like about it? I know it's cold, but the blankets should help with that," she says gently, well-aware that if he discontinues dialysis, he will die.

Yesterday, I saw him return from dialysis in what looked like a hotel's giant black laundry bin of bedding, only his tired, pale face, wreathed by white towels, peeked out.

"No...it's boring," he shrugs. I've pitched passing the time on an iPad or a Nook, or by watching TV or napping, to no avail.

She stares at him in disbelief. "Well, I haven't heard that one before."

After a beat, she asks softly, "John, would you say you're feeling depressed?"

The father mask that he has always worn around me drops, revealing a sad, vulnerable elderly man I've never met.

"Yeah. I feel pretty low," he says softly.

"Do you miss Dawn?"

He looks down. "Yeah."

Tears well up in my eyes as I encounter him with his defenses down, perhaps for the first time.

"I just don't feel...useful." His bony shoulders droop.

"But can you think of things you're looking forward to? Things you don't want to miss? I see your daughter's here," his doctor says, gesturing to me.

He searches for an answer, then looks over at me and laughs. "It's not like she's getting married soon or anything."

Ouch.

I look out the window behind me to hide my hurt reaction.

Don't take it personally, Susan, that you're not a good enough reason for your father to keep living. His physically-compromised life was just easier with Mom around.

The woman he'd taken a shine to stopped returning his calls, and a caregiver he found attractive yelled at him when he called her off the clock.

No wonder he's ready to call it quits.

"Well, then we'll get you information about your hospice options," the doctor says curtly, visibly annoyed with his disinterest in life-saving medical technology. "We can't release you, though, until you're over the C. diff infection you contracted while being here."

She swiftly exits, and Dad's eyelids get heavy.

I check the time on my phone. "I'm going to meet Anna at your apartment now, then she's going to come visit you," I say, knowing this old friend from church should cheer him up. "I'll be back later."

He nods with his eyes closed.

I exit his room and remove the head-to-toe plastic covering required for visiting a patient with C-diff, leaving me in my sandals, blue jeans, and gray T-shirt. I get in my car and decide to take the longer beach route to his place.

How often will I come here after Dad's gone?

I drive by the Santa Barbara Sunday art fair's idyllic setting: sunny summer day with a soft breeze, sparkling ocean stretching into the horizon, couples in white linen and large hats oohing and ahhing as they snake through captivating landscapes on easels.

How soon will Dad die without dialysis? Will he be in pain? Is he making this life-or-death decision in his right mind? There'll be so much to do after he's gone. What will my life be like without him?

Dad is my last, longest constant, and losing him will fully untether me from who I was and ever used to be. How interminable my conspiracy theory-filled afternoons with my parents felt at the time. At 36 years old, I now see our time together as achingly brief.

I park at Dad's retirement community, and all the way to his apartment, residents stop me and ask about him. They all know when one of their own has taken a turn.

While I arrange a plate of snacks in silence, I sense the eeriness of being in this apartment alone. It always feels like time stands still here. A faint knock instantly comforts me, and I open the door. Seeing Anna's warm, familiar face from my childhood takes me back to another life.

"Susan! It's been so long!" she squeals, just as upbeat as I remember her. Aside from longer and deeper wrinkles, she's exactly the same: thin, white blonde hair cut at her jawline that bounces every time she laughs her frequent chicken-like giggle. In loose, mismatched denim, she still has an eye twitch of frequent, strong blinking.

We sit at the breakfast table with crackers and cheese between us while sunlight from the patio creates a gold haze around the room. I'm comforted again when she says she knows what I'm going through.

"My mother died of kidney failure. She couldn't do dialysis either," she says, shaking her head, making her short hair sway. "We went into one of those clinics to check it out, saw all these old, pale people hooked up to machines, and my mom said it looked-" She lowers her voice to a whisper, and her eyes widen. "-like Night of the Living Dead." Then she lets out a cackle, and I laugh along with her.

"Yeah, Dad's doctor can't understand why he doesn't want to do it," I say, grabbing a cracker.

Suddenly, she becomes dead serious, a jolting pivot for someone always so sanguine.

"Susan, God put some things on my heart to tell you."

A faint panic flutters in my stomach, but I mentally override it.

I don't need to be afraid of this anymore.

"Before I continue, I want to know if you still believe in God, and if you're open to hearing what God has to say to you," she says, her thin lips tight and blue eyes laser-focused on me. Her aggressive blinking has miraculously stopped.

"I do not consider myself a Christian anymore," I say carefully, conscious of my goals to be both truthful and inoffensive to someone who's always been kind to me. But Christians have a way of putting you on the spot, don't they?

"I know, though, that you have my best interests at heart," I continue, "so I'm open to hearing anything you want to say." I sit back in my chair and smile cordially.

She pulls out a notepad from her enormous purse and puts on her red glasses. While they dangle on the edge of her nose, she reads, "Three things were put on my heart to say to you. The word 'renew.' Something is beginning again for you, re-starting. Secondly, the phrase 'use your voice.' God wants you to use the voice you have. And finally, as I was driving here, He gave me an image of a bird flying free. He wants you to be free," she says, earnestly.

Three thoughts pop into my head one by one:

When Dad dies, I'll finally be free from having to listen to exactly this type of religious bullshit.

What a horrible thing to think, Susan.

Wow. She's right.

"Well, thank you, Anna," I say slowly. "Those are all really good things."

If only we could share encouraging, evocative phrases without invoking the man in the sky.

"Does any of that resonate with you?" She takes her glasses off and cocks her head to the side. Back to being put on the spot.

"Well…yes. My life is starting anew in a few ways. I lost my job during the pandemic, the theme park show I did forever, so I've been working at a winery giving tours and doing tastings." I take a breath. "You never met my old boyfriend Cary, but we broke up just before the pandemic."

Was it the flat-earther in-laws, Cary, that drove you to drink and stray? Or was it that we both changed so much in our 11 years together? I'm still ashamed of the inexperienced, naïve person I was when we met, the one who couldn't or wouldn't see your flaws…

"Oh, I'm sorry to hear all that," Anna says.

"But I've been seeing someone a friend introduced me to. He's a really good guy," I say with a smile, picturing Paul, my storybook-tall, dark, and handsome new boyfriend, whose Elvis impression cracks me up on our hikes. I brought him recently to meet my dad at the hospital, and Dad informed Paul that 9/11 was an inside job. Some things never change.

"Maybe he's The One," I say to Anna with a nervous laugh, allowing myself to ponder marriage for the first time. Maybe it's because as a widower, he's proven marriage material. Maybe it's because I'm about to be family-less. Or maybe I'm finally comfortable enough in my skin to share my whole self with someone else.

"I'm also thinking about auditioning again, so yeah, 'renew' and 're-starting' are right on the money."

She nods and waits for the rest.

"As for 'use my voice,' hm." I look down, letting my long tawny blonde hair dangle, undyed for years now, and put a piece of cheese on a cracker. "Well, I have started writing a book about my parents." I take a bite.

"Oh, really?" she says, delighted. The book she's imagining, and the book I'm writing, are likely two different things.

"Yeah," I say while chewing. "And, in a lot of ways-"

…that I won't go into…

"-I feel more and more like a bird flying free." I swallow and smile.

She beams at me, and we catch up on her life until she leaves to visit Dad. I take the remaining cheese and crackers outside onto Dad's small patio, sit on a mauve cushy chair flanked by the flowers Mom always grew wherever we lived, pink begonias, and bask in the sun.

Renew…use your voice…fly free…

CHAPTER 37
DAWN

"AN END IS ONLY a beginning in disguise."
-Craig D. Lounsbrough

~36~

Three weeks later, I'm back on my parents' patio in the sun, but this time I'm boxing Mom's begonias to take to my home and dusting off the patio chairs to prep them for donating. I stop when I hear a knock at the door.

"Hospice," a man's voice says.

"Come on in," I call as I step inside.

A squat, stocky middle-aged man with a mask loosely hanging from one ear opens the door and walks in. "I'm here for the equipment," he says unenthusiastically.

"Yes, there are two things. Both are in the bedroom this way."

I walk us back to Dad's sparse bedroom, where my colorful "Welcome home!" sign still hangs from when he returned from the hospital so he could die at home.

"The bed with guardrails is from hospice, and so is the commode," I say, pointing to each.

He starts breaking down the bed into pieces he can carry out.

I sit at Dad's desk and wearily eye the daunting stack of mail. One by one, I set most aside to discard, but one envelope catches my eye.

"How's your day goin'?" the man asks while he loudly disconnects the metal pieces of the bed frame.

"Okay," I sigh, not looking over at him.

I don't want to talk about it.

"You?" I deflect.

"Well, they tried to hold me up at the front desk again. They want everyone who comes in here to be vaccinated, and I have to stand up for my rights every time," he growls.

My ears heat up.

Maybe this place is just trying to protect its vulnerable, elderly residents from dying, asshole!

"So, then they ordered me to wear a mask even though they have no right to. They've got a lot of-"

"Look, my dad died today, and I'd rather not talk about that right now," I say sharply without looking over at him. The call that I'd been keeping my phone on full volume for came just after two this morning.

"Suit yourself," he says with an unsympathetic shrug. In silence, he removes the hospice equipment piece by piece, and I'm relieved when he's gone.

Is everyone polarized by politically weaponized conspiracy theories now?

I shudder recalling the horror of watching election deniers storm the Capitol six months ago.

Yes. Yes, they are.

I wade through overstuffed donation bags in the living room to get to the bookcase to tackle next. The top shelf is jam-packed with binders in shades of maroon, navy, and forest green. I open them and discover that each is filled with printed out Bible verses related to healing and Dad's passionate meditations on them:

"...JAMES 5:15 'And the PRAYER OF FAITH will SAVE THE

ONE WHO IS SICK, and the LORD WILL RAISE HIM UP.' THIS IS MY PRAYER OF FAITH!!! I WILL BE RAISED UP!!! YOU ARE THE ONE WHO HEALS THE SICK!!! ISAIAH 53:5 'But he was wounded for our transgressions, He was bruised for our iniquities…AND BY HIS STRIPES, WE ARE HEALED.' BY HIS STRIPES I AM HEALED!!!! YES, JESUS, THANK YOU THANK YOU THANK YOU!!!! I BELIEVE AND RECEIVE YOUR HEALING, LORD!!!!!…"

My heart lurches out of my chest seeing page after page and binder after binder filled with Dad's zealous pleas for a miracle that never occurred.

Are these the ravings of a madman? Or evidence of a profound, admirable faith?

Spirituality, unlike anything else, precariously straddles the line of fantasy/delusion, inspirational/insane. There's Mother Teresa, but there are also the murders recounted in *Under the Banner of Heaven* perpetrated by Mormon fundamentalists who claimed god told them to do it.

I was initially struck by the peace Dad's faith and promise of heaven provided him when he accepted that without dialysis, he would be at his end. *Is false hope better than none?* I wondered.

Then, his last week on Earth was a hell I wish on no one. With toxic blood, unfiltered by working kidneys, pulsing through his veins, he was out of his mind with anxiety and confusion and barely able to speak or move.

Maybe praying for healing was the only way he could hold onto his faith and cope with the inexplicable loss of his mobility.

After spoon-feeding him apple sauce a few days ago while his eyes darted and limbs shook until he struggled to yell "Stooooop!" when he was full, I screamed at the top of my lungs on the drive home to god or anyone out there to be merciful and end his suffering.

I guess we're all believers when we have nowhere else to turn.

With a heavy heart, I take Dad's anguish-filled papers out of the binders to recycle and put the empty binders in a donation box. One by one, I add the bookcase's Christian and health-related literature to the donation box, too. When I reach the flat earth books and a slim one titled *COVID-19 IS A HOAX!*, I march them into the kitchen and, with both hands, slam them into the trash. I feel like I just shed 50 pounds.

IT'S OVER.

Then I spot something else I threw in the trash and gag all over again.

When a hospice nurse went over Dad's current medications with me so she could have an updated list, she pointed to one pill bottle on the table with an odd expression.

"What about this one?" she asked tentatively.

I leaned in and squinted to read the cursive purple lettering on the white supplement bottle: "Horny Goat Weed."

"No!" I said quickly. I snatched it up to trash it, and just when I thought the moment couldn't get any more mortifying, I noticed a distinct lightness and lack of pills rattling inside. IT WAS EMPTY!

Does Christianity's no-sex-before-marriage rule apply when you're 78?

It didn't help when my therapist nonchalantly informed me how rampant sexual activity is at senior living homes.

No, Cindy, NO!

By early evening of my first day without a living parent, my muscles are sore and eyelids heavy. There's still much to do, but it's time to go home. Just before leaving, I go back to Dad's desk and grab the piece of mail I'd set aside: his completed ballot to recall the governor. Even though our votes will cancel each other out, I put it in my purse to mail.

Honor your father and mother.

I also grab the heavy white plastic bucket purposely misla-beled 'Tools' from the back of his closet that is filled with the gold and silver coins he hoarded for decades in preparation for a global market crash. I will exchange them for cash.

Honor yourself.

———

After several long days of emptying and cleaning my parents' last home, I stand at the door about to close it for the last time, between a past with them and a future without. My eyes wander the empty white walls, bare tan carpet, and twinkling patio lights gleaming in at dusk. While wispy hair falls from my messy bun and sweat dries in my gray sweats, Anna's impartations echo:

Renew.

Being intentionally present and hands-on for Dad's decline proved surprisingly healing for the open wound of regret I'd carried since losing Mom.

Use your voice.

Maybe my experiences can help others grow, laugh, and not feel alone.

Fly free.

I'm blessed with the love and support of my chosen family of friends and Paul, the man I'm going home to, the man I might...

I switch the empty apartment's light off, and the shoebox-sized living room turns into a small black box theatre. Like rainbow flashes, sped-up scenes with my parents here and elsewhere flicker before my eyes, holograms moving at the accelerated pace and heightened emotions of a silent movie. I breathe in and smile before closing the door for good.

I'm just grateful for the time we had together.

ACKNOWLEDGMENTS

A mountain of a thank you goes to my very first reader, Andrew Diego, who waded through the firstest of drafts and did the nitty-grittiest of clean-up work. Thank you to my second reader, Kelly Bailey. The hours-long conversation we had about religion and family after is something I will always cherish. To my third reader, Joan Afton: your notes, "more, more, more!" were invaluable in showing me where I needed to expand. To my fourth reader, Peter Allen Vogt, thank you for your thoughtful notes and perfect punch-ups. Thank you to Bill Lewis for engaging in a memoir-reading swap!

A huge thank you to the Berkeley Writers Circle Meetup group for over a year of spot-on critiques and encouragement.

For their invaluable advice on the book business, I would like to thank Melody Stanford, Nadine Semereau, Mike Kalinowski, Beth Curry, Nathan Makaryk, Dan Bronson, Grant Merritt, Dave Razowsky, and Michael McIlwee.

Thank you, Chris Raymond and Marco Gomez, for permitting me to use lyrics from their musical *Dorian's Descent*. And thank you, Alisha Soper, for the brilliant "MOMoir!"

Thank you to the family and friends who shared their insights and memories about my parents, and thank you to everyone who I gave a heads-up about being mentioned in the book for your positive and supportive replies.

And finally, thank you, Paul, for your constant love, support, and sense of adventure. #WeGotMarried!

ABOUT THE AUTHOR

Susan Huckle is an actor in Los Angeles, but that wasn't self-indulgent enough, so she wrote a memoir. She grew up in Santa Maria, CA, and earned her B.A. in Journalism and Dramatic Art from the University of North Carolina at Chapel Hill, as well as a Master of Sustainable Tourism from Arizona State University. Her TV credits include *Jane the Virgin*, *The Mindy Project*, and Nickelodeon shows, and she's no stranger to most theatres in L.A. May you continue to work towards peace with yourself and those important to you, as she has done by writing this.

instagram.com/suzhuc